the story within

New Insights and Inspiration for Writers

Laura Oliver, M.F.A.

ALPHA

A member of Penguin Random House LLC

ALPHA BOOKS

Published by Penguin Random House LLC

Penguin Random House LLC, 375 Hudson Street, New York, New York 10014, USA • Penguin Random House LLC (Canada), 90 Eglinton Avenue East, Suite 700, Toronto, Ontario M4P 2Y3, Canada (a division of Pearson Penguin Canada Inc.) • Penguin Books Ltd., 80 Strand, London WC2R 0RL, England • Penguin Ireland, 25 St. Stephen's Green, Dublin 2, Ireland (a division of Penguin Books Ltd.) • Penguin Random House LLC (Australia), 250 Camberwell Road, Camberwell, Victoria 3124, Australia (a division of Pearson Australia Group Pty. Ltd.) • Penguin Books India Pvt. Ltd., 11 Community Centre, Panchsheel Park, New Delhi—110 017, India • Penguin Random House LLC (NZ), 67 Apollo Drive, Rosedale, North Shore, Auckland 1311, New Zealand (a division of Pearson New Zealand Ltd.) • Penguin Books (South Africa) (Pty.) Ltd., 24 Sturdee Avenue, Rosebank, Johannesburg 2196, South Africa • Penguin Books Ltd., Registered Offices: 80 Strand, London WC2R 0RL, England

004-189929-November2011

International Standard Book Number: 978-1-61564-114-7
Library of Congress Catalog Card Number: 2011905821

17   16   15   8   7   6

Interpretation of the printing code: The rightmost number of the first series of numbers is the year of the book's printing; the rightmost number of the second series of numbers is the number of the book's printing. For example, a printing code of 11-1 shows that the first printing occurred in 2011.

Printed in the United States of America

Note: This publication contains the opinions and ideas of its author. It is intended to provide helpful and informative material on the subject matter covered. It is sold with the understanding that the author and publisher are not engaged in rendering professional services in the book. If the reader requires personal assistance or advice, a competent professional should be consulted.

The author and publisher specifically disclaim any responsibility for any liability, loss, or risk, personal or otherwise, which is incurred as a consequence, directly or indirectly, of the use and application of any of the contents of this book.

Trademarks: All terms mentioned in this book that are known to be or are suspected of being trademarks or service marks have been appropriately capitalized. Alpha Books and Penguin Random House LLC cannot attest to the accuracy of this information. Use of a term in this book should not be regarded as affecting the validity of any trademark or service mark.

Most Alpha books are available at special quantity discounts for bulk purchases for sales promotions, premiums, fund-raising, or educational use. Special books, or book excerpts, can also be created to fit specific needs.

For details, write: Special Markets, Alpha Books, 375 Hudson Street, New York, NY 10014.

For Clay
with love and gratitude
and for Audra, Andrew, and Emily;
my first and best stories,
my inspiration now and always.

Contents

Introduction

Early September. The evening light lingers dry and clear now that autumn is calling the leaves from the tulip poplars. Dry as paper, they scatter before me as I walk across campus to my first writing workshop of the semester. Greeting the security guard who nods in return, I run up the steep steps of Barr-Buchanan.

I am on time, but my students are already in their seats as I enter the room. Undergraduates, graduate students, and members of the community encircle the polished oak table. They are glowing with hope, dampened by doubt. They've gambled tonight, paid actual money for a class that won't give them a marketable skill and may in fact require self-disclosure and fortitude. They will introduce themselves with goals about novels and memoirs, yet each will harbor a hidden agenda.

Sometimes the longing to write is an unacknowledged feeling in need of conscious expression. A young nurse last semester who was also a wife and mother of three discovered that healing others had become a burden too great to bear. "Every day I walk home looking for places to put my secrets," she wrote. "Intimacies shared with the dying, secrets no one wants to know."

Sometimes it's about the need for attention. The charming retired physician who forgot to bring his assignment to class suggested he recite it from memory. Eyes closed as if channeling, chin raised, he began. Fifteen minutes later, I had to laugh at his ingenuity. His story had no end because he was making it up as he went along.

Tonight, as always, it will be about self-awareness. The beautiful girl with the pierced brow has been to the hospital seven times in the last semester, each time certain she was going to die. The essay she reads aloud will not be about compulsion as one might expect, but about the tenacity of her parents' love.

Sometimes the longing to write is a search for self-worth—a way of saying to the world, "I am here." A boy with huge eyes at the end of the table this evening can barely whisper his name. I hope he'll discover that what astronomer Martin Rees observed about planets beyond our solar system is true of human nature as well: not everything that's interesting shines.

As we go around the table making introductions, most students claim they have come for discipline. What they mean is they've come *to be* disciplined. They confess their lack of productivity as if it's a character flaw, seeking to have their creativity forced from them by assignments. They picture class as a kind of writing boot camp and they are ready to suffer, but motivation produces the same results. Their desire and experience swirl like atoms in a solar birth. It is inspiration, not discipline, that ignites the core.

Over the next 10 weeks, as my students begin to put themselves on the page, I will be humbled again and again by the richness of the human spirit and the deceptiveness of its packaging. A quiet, middle-age woman writes of searching the world over for a place to leave the ashes of her teenage son. The family flies to Ireland seeking ancestral ground and finds a centuries-old monument in a secluded Irish glen. Realizing they've found the resting place of an ancient boy king, the family leaves behind the ashes and a piece of each member's heart. As my student reads her essay, a piece of us is left there, too. What we witness in words changes who we are.

"Can essays be funny?" a student asks, and I say yes. Writing a humorous essay requires the same skill that writing a poignant one requires: the willingness to convict yourself, to be surprised by your subject. Real subjects reveal themselves; if you pursue them, they disappear. The truth is that I have never met a student without a story, but I have rarely met a student who recognized from the outset what it was.

After more than a decade of teaching writing, I know that my students seek connection—to themselves and to others. To achieve this, they are going to need to relinquish preconceived notions.

"We're not here for you to write what you know," I say, which sounds heretical. "The truth is no one cares what you know. Your authority isn't credible, but your vulnerability is. Become brave, become curious. Whether you are writing fiction or essay, readers are interested in what you *don't* know but would like to. At our most basic level, we all have the same questions."

"Try this," I say. "Finish this sentence as many times as you can: 'What scares me is _____.' Or 'The mystery is _____.' Write with abandon, write down whatever comes to mind, quickly; don't stop to think about it or censor your response."

A hand shoots up. "How many words does it have to be?"

Sometimes you can throw open the cell door and the prisoner won't budge.

The most significant thing my students don't know about learning to write could transform their lives. For now, we will start with this simple truth: *you don't have to know where you are going in order to begin.*

It's a new thought, and I watch them process it. Not knowing where your story will end offers both freedom and risk, but they're ready to explore. As John A. Shedd is often quoted, "A ship in the harbor is safe, but that is not what ships are built for."

Acknowledgments

My heartfelt thanks to my wise and gentle editor Randy Ladenheim-Gil for shepherding this book with remarkable generosity and to Lori Hand for her editorial guidance as well. Thanks to Marie Butler-Knight for her expertise and to the entire production team at Alpha Books/Penguin. My gratitude to Alice Mattison, my gifted mentor and friend, and to Brian Doyle, Cynthia Gorney, Scott Russell Sanders, and Howard Norman; thank you for so generously sharing your work.

My sincere appreciation to all those talented writers who shine from within these pages: Paul Beckman, Betty Driscoll, Dena Elliott, Alan Elyshevitz, Ann Jensen, Doris Kamenetz, Chang Liu, Patrick Madden, Barbara Klein Moss, Andrew C. Oliver, Hank Pugh, Camilla Schwarz, Sarah Jo Sinclair, Jeanne Slawson, Tom Woodward, and Linda Woolford. My gratitude to Mark Bailey, Iain Baird, Seth Clabough, Jane Elkin, Margaret Foster, Jon Franklin, Nadja Maril, Trey Miller, Hank Parker, Ellen Santasiero, Lynn Schwartz, Brenda Wintrode, Henriette Leanos, and Mary Ann Treger for their valuable contributions as well. My thanks to my students at St. John's College, the University of Maryland, Baltimore County, and The Writer's Center. It is a privilege to hear your stories.

Thank you to my mother, Virginia Pritchett, for all those years of reading stories aloud and all those trips to the library.

To my husband, Clay, my heartfelt appreciation for supporting my efforts, writing and otherwise, and for laughing in all the right places (writing and otherwise). Audra, Andrew, and Emily, words fail me. Thank you for giving me stories to tell.

Part 1
Getting Started

1

Why We Write, Why We Don't

"A year from now you'll wish you had started today."
—Karen Lamb

"In the end, love—withheld or offered, lost and sought after—is the story, again and again," observes Meredith Hall. When we're writing about conflict or events that scared us, it may not feel as if we are writing about love, but according to Natalie Goldberg, it is also our motive. Our deepest secret, she says, is that we write because we love the world. Ultimately we are telling one story.

On New Year's Day afternoon, my son Andrew, not quite a toddler at the time, was scooting around the family room in a walker while my husband Clay and I dismantled the Christmas tree. Ice pelted the windows, sand against glass, as wind-driven snow stormed outside.

When my friend Ann called, I took a break, perching on a wicker stool in the kitchen to catch up while Clay continued removing ornaments from the tree. Andrew lurched about in the walker, amusing himself as the snow outside accentuated the glowing fire in the fireplace and the sense of well-being inspired by a family at home together.

I was aware of Andrew but peripherally, the way you are conscious of traffic on the other side of the road, when he careened to a halt in front of my stool, suddenly gasped, and half stood.

A strange rigidity gripped his body, as if a voice had just whispered, "I have something to tell you," and I, too, froze in that ominous pause. Within seconds, Andrew's face lost its pink flush of health and began turning the color of stone.

I threw down the phone and called for Clay, who came running, a string of lights still dangling in his hand. He grabbed Andrew instinctively, in an attempt to lift him from the walker, but corduroy pants, a bulky diaper, and rubber tennis shoes conspired to tangle Andrew's legs in the canvas strapping.

"Get an ambulance," Clay called out as he struggled to free our son. I turned toward the phone as if underwater. It seemed like miles from where I stood to the wall where it hung. Behind me the walker fell away with a clatter as Clay freed Andrew and turned him headfirst toward the floor. I watched myself lift the receiver then and dial 911. I had been talking all afternoon, why the ominous silence now? Outside the disinterested snow blew higher against the sills. With rising panic, I realized the line was dead.

As I watched Clay struggle to open our son's mouth, I re-experienced Andrew's brief life in an instant download of memory. Not the joy of his smile or the sweetness of his voice—it was the morning sickness, diaper changes, and sleepless nights I experienced once again, and the thought that came unbidden as my son's life slipped away was shocking in its neutrality:

All that hard work ... for nothing.

As a mother, my dispassionate response was a shock. As a writer, it was a mystery I had to explore on the page, so I gave the same crisis and reaction to a mother in a short story. By imagining the husband's explanation of the mother's detachment, I realized why, in reality, I had shut down.

"I'm a fake, I'm a freak. I don't love my own baby," the mother says, and her husband, who is leaving her, knows in his heart that's not true.

"It's just easier to leave than be left," he says.

In reality, Clay desperately continued his efforts to clear Andrew's airway and moments later, pulled the jagged metal cap to a glass Christmas tree ornament from his throat, the splayed wire prong still attached. Andrew's face turned pink and, able to breathe again, he began to howl. Now safe, he could voice his fear until it became something else—blustering astonishment at the indignity of what had just happened to him.

It has been years since this incident happened, and I admit the truth of the moment as only that. As a writer, if you are using your own experiences to enrich your work, be careful of turning those moments into conclusions about your character. It wouldn't be fair, and you would most likely be wrong. Passing judgment on anyone in your work is an error.

Reasons We Write

"Writing is the process by which you explain to yourself what happened to you," Arlene Croce says, but there are many other reasons to write. Write because you are a witness, not just to events, but to what mattered about those events. Not just to relationships, but to how those relationships exposed or celebrated a truth. Write because you are an explorer of yourself and of the human condition. Write to cherish what will otherwise be lost and to understand what has never made sense. The more personal your discovery, the more universal it is. For instance, in the moment I saw Andrew begin to wail once he could breathe again, I realized how common it must be to hide fear beneath anger. I realized the husband in my piece of fiction was doing just that as well—leaving because it was less frightening than confrontation.

You write to entertain and, in fiction, to stretch the imagination, to incorporate what you've experienced with what you can envision.

And you write for connection: to yourself, to humanity, to something greater than yourself.

Edgar Mitchell, who was part of the Apollo 14 mission to the moon, speaks of suddenly understanding that there is a connection between everything in the universe on the return flight to Earth—a connection between the particles in his body, and the members of his team, to the rocket itself. "I was manufactured in some earlier generation of stars," he says in the movie *In the Shadow of the Moon*. Writing expresses that feeling—that we are connected at our origin in the dust of ancient stars. As you search for a subject, know you can write about anything if you do it well. According to Bill Roorbach in *Writing Life Stories*, sixteenth-century French aristocrat Michel de Montaigne, commonly regarded as the father of the modern essay, developed an intense friendship with Etienne de la Botie. The two young men were kindred spirits, intellectuals with similar sensibilities. They examined the world in continuous conversation until the dialogue abruptly ended with Etienne's untimely death at the age of 32.

Devastated at his loss, the grieving de Montaigne continued his conversations with his friend by writing candid and personal vignettes, each an *essai*, French for "to try" or "a small attempt." De Montaigne wrote of all the mundane things two friends might have mused about, from drunkenness to vanity. We still read these essays. As H. L. Mencken said, "There are no dull subjects. There are only dull writers." In addressing such ordinary subjects, de Montaigne created the equivalent of informal snapshots of the man he was, as opposed to a formal portrait done in oils, and we received a new genre—personally revealing, universally appealing.

Anne Lamott, novelist and essayist, writes of stumbling—as a mother, a friend, and a human being. As she writes of her failure to get off a ski lift, she teaches us that it is okay to fall, that no one gets up or down life's mountains unscathed. Our flailing, Lamott shows us, is the first step in surrendering to grace. Scott Russell Sanders, also a critically acclaimed essayist, writes of trying to show his young son Haley's Comet in a night thick with stars. Sanders points, guides, and directs his son's search, even as he realizes words can only point in a particular direction. We can't see the world through someone else's eyes.

So give yourself permission to write about anything that comes to you. To be paralyzed by lack of a subject or to wait for an idea will only prove this: *No one hates himself more than a writer who isn't writing*.

And Why We Don't Write

If the longing to write is so common for so many, why is it so difficult to do? My students have the usual theories: not enough time, kids, interruptions, work pressures, or lack of privacy or place. While those issues are factors, none of them are the real culprit.

Most people don't write because on some subtle, subconscious level, they believe their efforts must be perfect. Procrastination protects perfectionism's version of reality: "When I *do* get around to it, it's going to be *spectacular!*"

Everyone has internalized a personal critic (PC) to some degree. It is the voice in your head that tells you your pants are too short, or you left the dinner party too late, or no one has ever heard of your college. "Just one more thing," the PC whispers, tapping you on the shoulder. "You're too lazy, too undisciplined, and too *late* to be a writer." The PC wants to help this sink in. "This is good," it reasons, pulling up a chair to stay a while, "because you have no ideas, no original experiences, and anything you might write about has already been published by someone else." The PC knows your creative spirit is a vulnerable child and thinks that mocking, criticizing, and intimidating that child will protect it from pain and humiliation. The PC feels like a disapproving parent, which makes it particularly insidious because parents are supposed to protect us, right? ("Don't run with that stick. Don't put bobby pins in the light sockets.") The PC takes your creative child hostage and you bond with the kidnapper.

The PC is a perfectionist when perfection isn't a reasonable expectation. Why should you be able to write skillfully crafted and entertaining stories from the get-go, when even learning to bake from a mix results in some cakes that don't rise? As Henriette Anne Klauser points out in *Writing on Both Sides of the Brain*, your first verbal attempts at language were cheered on and encouraged. Your first attempts at writing were *corrected*.

Your critic's energy is your anxiety. It is addicted to past and future. It shows up at your doorstep like a missionary thrusting doomsday literature into your hand. "The World Is Going to End!" reads the headline. There is an illustration of the Saved in a lifeboat and wait … isn't that you? Floundering in the waves hanging on to … oh yes, a pen. Thank your anxiety for its effort and close the door. After all, what is anxiety but fear? And fear but lack of faith? And lack of faith, a lack of trust? And what can you do about it?

Building a Writing Life

If you were bringing a newborn home from the hospital, would you walk in and drop the baby on the sofa? Would you say to your spouse "Just put that thing anywhere" and wander off to the kitchen? If you had bought a new Tesla Roadster, a sporty little number with a price tag north of $100,000, would you park it on the street?

The creative spirit wants what we all come into the world wanting: to be nurtured and protected, to love and to be loved. Find a place in your home that is just for your writing, not where you pay the bills or do anything else that feels like a chore. Make it a place you can quiet the mind and listen. And because nature is inherently inspiring, make it a place with a window if possible. However you design it, this place is to be your writing sanctuary.

Make it more than one place. Upstairs and down, inside and out. Make it a place that always evokes a sense of well-being. Arrange photos of those you love along with tokens of success and affection near your desk. Paint the room a color that makes you smile every time you walk in. Surround yourself with books you enjoy, writers whose voices inspire you, or reference books that instruct. Maybe there is something from your childhood on your desk. Among the items on my own desk, I have a small wooden rooster carved for me when I was 16 by a boy in Appalachia where I was working on a humanitarian project. The poverty and isolation of his mountain community was a revelation. It took the youth group I was with five hours to travel the last 100 miles.

We arrived in the midst of a monarch butterfly migration and the hills of Morris Fork were draped in a fluttering orange curtain of billowing wings. Every tree, every fence post, every wheelbarrow was blanketed. As we staggered stiff from the car, clouds of butterflies rose and alighted on our arms and shoulders, hands and legs, adorning us with their fragility. The carved rooster reminds me that once I was willing to work very hard and travel very far to be of service to someone other than myself, which still sounds like an excellent plan. So choose tokens for your desk that anchor you to the positive, that reflect your best moments and draw more similarly positive energy to you.

Be sure you make the distinction between items that genuinely evoke a positive feeling and those that you think *should* make you feel good. This is a subtle and tricky business. It requires bare-bones honesty. Yes, you love that vacation house where you fly-fish in Idaho, but if the mortgage is killing you, it's not such a good choice.

Yes, you love your daughter and that's a gorgeous photo of her, but if, in reality, it was taken when your relationship was at a low point, chances are you need to choose something else. Your writing space must be an authentic reflection of all that *feels* good, all that makes you like yourself, all that reminds you that when you subtract your mood and the pettiness of most things that bother you, life is a gift.

Sharing Work

It is wonderful to share your work, but only with the right person. Ideally this is someone with a similar sensibility, someone who respects and likes you and is in no way in competition with you. If that person is another writer, you will be able to ask for insights as to craft, but you must both deeply believe in a universe of abundance— that success breeds success—and that one person's good fortune enhances the probability of another's good fortune. You will know immediately upon sharing work whether you have chosen your reader well. You will either feel inspired ("Brilliant! I can't wait to make that change.") or discouraged ("Oh, well ... I can still start a home repair business ... maybe sell stuff on eBay ..."). If your reader inspires you, even by doing something as simple as asking to see another story, you may have found an invaluable sounding board that you will use throughout your writing life. If you feel diminished in any way, honor your feelings and find a new reader.

When I first began writing essays, a new and hugely enthusiastic friend asked to see my work. I was flattered and excited to share. I gave her an essay about a disastrous afternoon with my then 8-year-old daughter. It was a piece about incubating birds' eggs in a fragile nest. It was a piece about excitement and anticipation. It was also a piece about a horrific accident, and a broken yellow yolk sliding off a child's canvas shoe. It was a piece about a child so frozen in remorse and embarrassment I thought she might never make another spontaneous movement for the rest of her life as she walked, rigid and regal, to the car. There, she arranged herself with careful formality on the front seat next to me and stared in silence out the window all the way home. I loved the piece and I hoped my friend would love it, too, because, of course, it was really about how fiercely we long to protect our children and their dreams and how utterly impossible it is to do so.

My friend did love the piece. She was so enthusiastic that she ran over the next day to return my essay, line-edited with a red pen. In a burst of goodwill, she had marked up the entire story with her improvements, then given it to her husband, an out-of-work artist, to mark up as well. I suspect they had even given their 6-year-old a go at it. It was wounded, in need of triage. There may have been some wonderful insights in their editing, but what they gave back was so different from what I'd been seeking, I couldn't look.

When you share your work, *ask for exactly what you are seeking*. If all you want is for the other person to see what you've been up to or to offer encouragement, say that. Sometimes you want to share the energy but the work is too tender, too new, to expose to another's viewpoint. If you want to know if the writing is clear but don't want input on your subject, say that. If you want a line edit, say that. And whatever you get back, view it with a discerning eye. Some feedback is invaluable, inspiring; other feedback can be just plain bad advice, perhaps the result of less than careful reading. Learn to recognize what is of value, be grateful for it, and let the rest go.

Don't give your unwritten or unpublished work a title and parade it around. It will tire and so will you. It is a little like leasing a car and pretending you own it. Don't over-talk your story. You will dilute its potency.

Join an organization of writers for support and companionship, ideas, jobs, or a way to get away from the computer but still be nurturing your writing. Consider joining a critique group if the chemistry feels right, but as with everyone else with whom you share work, it's a date, not a marriage. Give yourself a graceful out. "I'm not sure how collaborating will work for me. Let's experiment for a couple of months and see how it goes."

Your job is to improve your writing in a way that feels good.

Suffering is not part of the program.

Sabbaticals and Pressure

You do not need a sabbatical from your role as a parent, a son, an employee, a friend, or a spouse in order to write. In fact, such open blocks of time are accompanied by so much expectation that they can become pitfalls. Time raises the ante so high that inspiration tends to fold her hand and forfeit the pot.

Your life is grist for the mill. Live it, and fit your writing into your routine in a way that feels reasonable. Ease into a pattern that works for you and avoid the diet and exercise mentality of chastisement and guilt. Train yourself to drop in and out of your work even if it is only for 15 or 20 minutes at a time. If the only time you have to write is while the baby is napping or on Saturday mornings before the weekend chores take precedence, learn to use those opportunities.

On the days you can't write, just take notes. Once you have committed to a writing life, you see the world differently. By just noting what you observe, you can still work on your writing, even on the days you can't get to the page.

What page are you on? Nonwriting friends often ask this question as a measure of progress (yours) and judgment (theirs), and it ramps up your own expectations in ways that don't serve you. The question is often followed by, "How long do you expect your book to be?" and a quick mental calculation. At this point it becomes clear that you are failing in some way.

Know that even one good paragraph a day is reason to celebrate. Set small goals. Make them smaller. Allow yourself to write badly in order to write at all. Really, really badly; just write. Know that you can chip away what doesn't shine later and quite possibly discover a jewel.

Absolutely reward yourself for your writing time. Give yourself something to look forward to: an hour to browse through the latest sports equipment catalog, lunch with a friend, or take your morning writing with you and go out for a cappuccino in the afternoon where you can sit in a fresh new location and review your progress. Buy snapdragons in January for your desk, a new mystery novel, a new mouse pad. Call a friend.

Inspiration

Take a class. Meet with another writer. Find a new author who is writing material that speaks to you. Create a shelf in your office for the works of authors you love, books on craft, and books of interesting facts. Listen to some jazz, blues, or Gregorian chants. Go for a walk.

We'll explore the role of the brain in facilitating creativity throughout this book, and the specialization of each brain hemisphere specifically in Chapter 4. Generally speaking, it is the right half of your brain that has a predilection for seeking patterns and finding resemblances. Ignite the creative spark in any discipline or art form and it will ignite the urge to write. Edward de Bono, author of *Lateral Thinking, Creativity Step by Step*, calls this phenomenon "cross-disciplinary fertilization." Explore books on unrelated topics: yacht design, buried treasure, lost cities, Sufi wisdom, pulsars, the Big Bang, Mayan cities, prehistoric cave paintings, lost manuscripts, particle accelerators and the origins of the universe, mind reading—whatever intrigues you. And do so with a notebook or computer nearby.

You can't continue to make withdrawals from your creative bank account without making deposits as well. This means replenishing the source of your creativity with new scenes, new people, and new experiences of all kinds. Visit art galleries or the SPCA, take a tour boat around the harbor, go on an historic tour of your own town, poke around marine supply stores or New Age stores, get your fortune told or your horoscope charted, go for a drive to the country or the city, take the metro, or go to the dog park. The human brain loves *new*. We may be the only species on the planet that immediately scans our environment for change.

If you live by the water, visit the mountains. Author Julia Cameron thinks of this process as having a date with your inner artist, an excursion for which you don't need or even want company. It is true that when you are with someone else, your energy is diverted to your companion when you need to be immersed in experience. Like driving while on a cell phone: sure you *can* do it, but can you really say you are connected to the task at hand? This is a time you need to be absorbing your surroundings, not making conversation. Still, a friend often takes us to unfamiliar territory, so embrace companionship when it means a new adventure.

Choosing Your Audience

Don't try to figure out at the outset who your intended reading audience is. It will interfere with your freedom of expression. You need to write the way you let toddlers pick out their own clothes for the day. Yes, the green cotton shorts may seem an odd choice to pair with the wool mittens, and the tiara may be a bit over the top, not to mention the red galoshes, but what style! What originality! Let your inner writer dress in anything he or she chooses; you can modify the outfit for the occasion after the fact. Write with freedom; save discernment for editing. You can reshape, add and delete, change a location—whatever is necessary once you have captured the words.

Another way to open the floodgates of expression is to write to the page as if the page itself is a person—a living, breathing being in whom you are confiding. Literally make the page your confidant, your listening ear. Interact with the page the way a model plays to a camera. She is posing for a piece of equipment, an inanimate visual recording instrument, but she interacts with it as if it is a portal through which she is connecting with observers on the other side. She imagines the camera is a person and projects herself into it. You can imagine the page is a person and project yourself *onto* it.

E-Mails and Blogs

If the idea of writing an essay or story is intimidating, try writing an e-mail. An e-mail is an absolutely painless point of entry to a narrative. E-mails are casual, easy forms of communication that allow you to simply talk on the page as if to a best friend. Life is a story. In an e-mail, you inevitably tell a tale about your day, about someone you know, about something that has happened. You can delete, cut and paste, and even look up words in order to find a better one with the touch of a key. E-mail is to essay as fuzzy slippers are to 6-inch heels.

If you begin to find your voice—a subject—you can even start a blog. A friend of mine started a blog that became quite popular. Eventually she turned her blog into an entire book.

You have so many points of entry available. Try them on and see which one fits.

It Is Already Tomorrow

The phone is ringing and I hope it is Andrew. The boy we almost lost on that long-ago January afternoon when winds downed the power lines is a young man now. He lives as far from snow as possible, 12,000 miles away on a pristine beach in New Zealand. His visits are so rare that he has never seen the house we now live in. He is, in fact, *so* far away that his spring is our fall and to calculate the time difference before I call him, I have to count eight hours backward and make it tomorrow.

I have told him the story of how he scared us, of how my love contracted in terror to become one detached thought, but the truth is this: I still wonder if he will be taken from us too soon, surfing alone off a rocky coast, driving too fast with unreliable brakes. I remind myself that writers' daydreams drift to drama; that this is not premonition but the work of the muse.

"I have this theory that anything that happens to you that leaves you alive and intact can be used somewhere in your writing," says Octavia Butler, and I hope this is true.

I pick up the phone and there is the briefest pause, as if the universe is taking a breath. Then his words bounce up from a sandy beach to starry satellites. They pass across seas and continents, deserts and forests, relayed by a series of universal transmitters to where I stand in a kitchen he's never seen.

The impulse to write is held in that pause, and love is the only story.

2

Point of Origin

"Creation, whatever its form, is not an act of will, but an act of faith."
—Lloyd Alexander

Things once in contact remain in contact through all space and all time, according to evidence compiled by science journalist Lynne McTaggart in *The Field: The Quest for the Secret Force of the Universe*. She is referring to the inexplicable but undeniable capability of quantum particles to affect each other at the speed of light across the vastness of space—the capability of two things to stay connected and able to communicate without visible means for all time. Unable to comprehend how this is possible, Albert Einstein ultimately called the phenomenon "spooky action at a distance." Writers call it inspiration.

Science is to literature what fuel is to flame.

What quantum mechanics is proving is that everything with mass (you, your dog, your desk) is at its most elemental level energy. It's easy to visualize. Take your hands off the keyboard and place them under a microscope and you'll see skin cells. But if you could increase the magnification to a high enough power, you'd see those cells are comprised of molecules and atoms. Atoms are comprised of neutrons, protons, and electrons, which are comprised of at least 50 progressively smaller particles like bosons and quarks. Ultimately, all that is left is an infinitely tiny vibrating particle of energy. What's miraculous is that the quantum particles of energy that comprise us, once in proximity, remain a part of each other for eternity. Quantum physics is proving what writers already know: that once two human lives have brushed against each other, they are forever linked. We explore this every day in novels, essays, and short stories.

Writers hear in metaphor, which means they find inspiration in virtually any subject. Still, if I had appreciated how closely related physics is to writing, I might have chosen it for my science requirement in college. But I chose biology (thinking it would be easier) which, in some kind of cosmic bait-and-switch, led to the dissection of things stored in formaldehyde.

Later I began to investigate physics on my own, not as a scientist but as a writer. I learned that an expanding universe allows us to retrace our trajectory to the place of our origin—the explosion of an infinitely dense, infinitely small point called a singularity. That point contained within it all the energy and matter that would ever exist.

The place where the entire known universe came into existence seems like a good place for stories to start.

Beginning Small and Dense

Start with the smallest, densest element you can. Something irreducible. A moment. An incident. Not "summer," not "last summer," but "one Thursday afternoon in late June just after the rain stopped." Bring it into focus by looking more and more closely. The key is to reduce these huge generalities to something specific. When you were in grade school, you were told to write essays on themes like freedom or democracy. Those were bland and uninspiring abstractions which could only produce bland generalizations. They were excruciating to write and worse to read. But when you made freedom an essay about the first time your mother let you walk home from school alone and you decided, in your 6-year-old logic, to drag a crayon down the sidewalk all the way from Lakeshore Elementary to your front door to sort of celebrate your new freedom and maybe make it *visible*, only walking six blocks hunched over with a crayon is harder than it sounds and you were late and your worried mother found you, brow furrowed, studiously backing your way toward home ... then it becomes something we can see and care about.

Or when democracy becomes not about governments but about who among your siblings sets the table, then you're off to the races. Keep reducing your focus until you finally reach an indivisible element, something specific.

Dena Elliott writes of such a moment in a hospital room with her father and in just 396 words, tells an entire story with a beginning, middle, end, and emotional take-away. First published in *The Sun* magazine, Dena writes of this singular incident in a way that also allows us to glimpse her family, their concern for each other, and their coping mechanisms under stress. Had she wanted to, she could have used the moment to launch an entire memoir.

Dena's father had been diagnosed with a tumor which was going to require brain surgery. The slightest error and her father could be left blind or worse.

The morning of the surgery our family sat in a hospital holding room aware that this could be the last time the four of us would be together.

"I hope this doctor got a good night's sleep," Dad joked. "If I'm a goner, will I even know it?"

"More important, how will we know it?" I said.

"Let's have a secret password," Dad suggested. "If I feel normal when I come out of the anesthesia, I'll say the password."

"How about 'fire truck'?" I said.

During the surgery, another family awaits news in the same alcove of the hospital. Their family member is having the same surgery, at the same time, but performed by a different doctor. Each family is periodically updated as the surgeries progress. Dena's family hears that her father's operation is going well. The other family does not get such good news.

> *Finally a nurse told us we could go in to see my father, one at a time. I walked slowly down the corridor. No matter what I found at the end, I knew my life was already changed. I would never again complain about my job. I wouldn't sweat the lack of groceries. I would hug my friends and family more often.*

> *Looking through the glass door of Dad's ICU room, I was horrified to see him staring at the ceiling and talking to himself. "He's talking to himself," I said to his nurse.*

> *"No, he's talking to you," she said. The nurse explained that his head was held in place, and he couldn't turn it, so he appeared to be speaking to no one. "Go on," she said.*

> *Because he'd had a breathing tube down his throat during the surgery my father could barely speak. I leaned down to say hello, and he whispered, "Fire truck, fire truck, fire truck."*

Expanding Your Entry

One of the most reliable methods for finding a subject by beginning with a single point is a universal tool with many names. The technique has been called clustering by Gabriele Lusser Rico in *Writing the Natural Way* and branching by Henriette Anne Klauser in *Writing on Both Sides of the Brain*. It is also often called brain-storming, rapid writing, free writing, or stream-of-consciousness writing. With practice, this is a reliable method for starting with a single point of entry and discovering a story.

Begin with one word, perhaps: "Sam," "St. Louis," or a general word chosen at random from a book or a dictionary, like "architecture" or "grievous," "transcendent" or "missing." It can be a word with which you already have a strong association or one with which you have no association at all. I have found Rico's method most effective at this point in the search for a subject.

Write the word in the middle of a piece of paper and circle it as if it is that infinitely dense point from which your story universe will expand. Circle the word until another word pops into your head. Draw a short line from your original word to the new word, and circle the new word. Continue to fill your paper with every single word that pops into your head, no matter how unrelated it may seem, linking each word with a line and always circling the new word until you come up with the next. Imagine you are mapping new galaxies, each revealing worlds you didn't know existed. As you land on each new world, you pause to refuel, then continue your exploration.

This kind of brainstorming is effective because these small motor movements keep your left brain in neutral, otherwise occupied, and your evocative right brain takes over, initiating the leap from one word to the next. The trick is to continue to go with the flow, quickly, without any second guessing, editing, or censoring. Your job at this point is to stay out of your own way and give your intuition free rein.

At some point, you will get a sense of sudden recognition—as if you have been scanning strangers on a subway platform and have suddenly spotted the person you have been looking for, or a person you recognize but are surprised and delighted to see.

At that point, as Rico explains, put the map aside and begin to write. Jump in and don't worry about having a perfect first sentence. Too often writers become paralyzed by thinking it has to be perfect or they won't get where they want to go. Leave that for the editing process. Write as long as you can, referring back to your original idea map when needed. You can open a short story, novel, or write an entire essay this way.

Each of these vignettes tends to intuitively become whole. Just continue to write until the piece feels complete, but if you need closure you can't find, as with any piece of writing, go back to the beginning and look at what you have given yourself to work with. Pick up a reference from your first page—the house in the rain, your mother's voice in the night, the key that did not fit the lock, the worn running shoes left by the door—and let that image recur as you close.

Small and specific story origins force you to stay concrete in fiction as well as in memoir, so begin with the boat ride, the phone call, the spilled coffee, and your story will grow on cause and effect. Even the largest of philosophical questions are best voiced in a small scene we can visualize. Hank Pugh's aptly titled piece of fiction, "One Morning in a Long Marriage," asks a huge question about the nature of love in a long-term commitment, but it turns on one moment, one gesture.

The story opens after Theo and his wife Grace have had an argument and gone to bed angry and silent, carefully arranging themselves in bed so that they will not touch even by accident. After a restless night, Theo awakes and wants only to escape to the river to be alone with his thoughts, to fish in the dawning light. Pugh writes:

By the time he had finished dressing, Theo assumed Grace was awake, though she did not stir as he approached her side of the bed. It seemed to him that whenever he was awake, Grace was awake; always awake, always watching. But as he bent to kiss her in the dawning light she did not offer her mouth, so he kissed her warm cheek, inhaling as he did her familiar scent. He turned to walk away, then stopped, wondering if what Grace had said last night was true. Was it true that sometimes you just have to go on in the absence of the proof of love, sometimes even in the absence of love itself?

He returned to her, knelt on one knee, laid his hand on her hip, and kissed her again. Though she was not awake to hear it, he made the small kissing sound that seemed to him necessary to complete the gesture.

This vignette can be considered complete, a scene that tells us where this couple has been and how they arrived where they are. But it can also become something larger because of its specificity. What happens next? Build on the connections that materialize as your character and his original situation expand. Where will Theo's need to complete gestures of love lead him?

Embrace the Blank Slate

So what if you sit down to write, and even with all these techniques for starting stories, your mind remains blank? Nothing seems to resonate. You're not feeling curious or inspired. In fact, the blank computer screen is making you anxious, even hostile. Celebrate. Applaud your recognition that being stuck is universal and no big deal. It doesn't mean you are not a writer. It means that you are.

Relax. Pick up another tool. Your memory and imagination weren't useful this time? Clustering and brainstorming didn't work? Then use description. Describe your fear, your frustration, or your curiosity about the blank page. When else have you felt this way? Write about it, or simply render the world around you in words. Describe the surface of your desk. What is on it? What is missing? Use sensory detail: Is it shiny? Rough? Smooth?

Describe your environment. Describe the cardinal on the holly tree outside your window. How is it that you learned to distinguish his call from the starling's call? Do you really know the voices of your own children, or do you jump every time a child calls out "Mom!" or "Dad!" in a mall? Does that make you less of a parent or more of one? Write absolutely anything because the truth is this:

It's the *physical* act of writing that inspires ideas. It's a biological response from your right brain (the artist) whenever your left brain (the logical litigator) is engaged. It's not necessary to wait for an idea to come first. Writing without inspiration, however self-consciously, primes the pump of imagination and memory. It signals to your inner writer, in ways both obvious and more subtle, that you are ready to receive.

Think of it like this: you're not trying to make up a story; you're trying to let the story within you get out. It's like running for the edge of a cliff with a hang glider. The run is awkward, you stumble a bit, you are burdened by your wings, but you keep running. At some moment, you're off! You are no longer straining for momentum but soaring on the wind. Maybe it will take you a page or more to know whether this story is going to stay aloft, but you can jettison your exploratory paragraphs later if they are unnecessary.

As you continue to write, details will begin to accrete; they will grow in depth and weight and take form. (The early emptiness of space contained little more than helium and hydrogen, but elements combined and recombined, and became something weighty and new.) Eventually characters will ignite and burn bright on the page. There, they will gravitate toward each other, which, interestingly, everything with mass tends to do.

An expanding universe means that someday there will be no stars in our sky. We'll be utterly, devastatingly alone. And yet, in the eternal paradox writers find so compelling, Lynne McTaggart's reporting predicts science also will prove this: "We never were alone. We were always part of a larger whole. We were and always have been at the center of things. Things did not fall apart, the center did hold, and it was we who were doing the holding."

3

Calling a Story to You: Subject

"My objective is to show what I found, not what I was looking for."
—Pablo Picasso

My name is Fabian Vas. I live in Witless Bay, Newfoundland. You would not have heard of me. Obscurity is not necessarily failure, though; I am a bird artist, and have more or less made a living at it. Yet I murdered the lighthouse keeper, Botho August, and that is an equal part of how I think of myself.

—Howard Norman, *The Bird Artist*

How do you find a subject? You find a subject by looking closely at other things: relationships, memories, mysteries, and conflicts. By looking at intriguing people and imagining what they might do under pressure. Clearly, there are as many variations on how to extract a story from experience and imagination as there are writers. One of the richest veins to mine for subject, however, is that place where we suddenly realize two contradictory statements or feelings are equally true, such as the quiet confession of Fabian Vas that he is both artist and murderer. How can two such opposite sensibilities be equally real? It's the kind of paradox that Hollywood uses to make robots' heads explode.

Exploring Contradictions

Contradictions are critical to writing. They are puzzles; the places we pause, places of intrigue, and places we reflect. They are also synonymous with conflict.

Contradictions are like the X on a treasure map that indicates, "stop and dig here." Where are they found? In feelings that don't make sense; in characters who make inexplicable choices. Observe your own life and take note of what you notice. Jot down the odd phrase or thought to explore. Keep a notebook in the car, by the bed. As you explore these thoughts later, get curious about discrepancies. Where is what you were expecting different from what you found? Recognize and respect these intersections. Contradictions will be found where something unpredictable happened, places where you were brought up short or surprised. Be willing to learn something new about a relationship or situation you thought you understood.

A contradiction can also be a Rosetta Stone, a means of translating the emotional truth of an experience from the event itself.

After my last child was born, I had the impulse to write but had lost all direction. It was as if I had packed my bags and was ready to go on a trip but didn't know what train to board. A writer friend suggested writing about the experience of having a child you know is your last.

The event was so recent, my memory so clear, the words came quickly. "They tell me to breathe, to ride the contraction like an ocean swell, cresting it in rhythmic control, but I barely hear them, diving deep beneath the pain. There is less movement in the depths, less distance to the shore."

My husband and I already had two children, a girl and a boy. So we had chosen, once again, to allow the baby's gender to remain a mystery and would be delighted with either one; a newborn daughter or son. In my heart of hearts, however, having sisters of my own, I may have had the slightest preference for another girl.

As I wrote of the delightful suspense before the doctor sang out, "It's a ... girl!" I stopped, confused. Revisiting that instant of joy, I realized I'd *felt* disappointment.

The realization made no sense but was an undeniable fact. Everything was right and yet I remembered a wave of sadness. You can't write for very long before the truth emerges and demands attention, so when contradictions arise you keep writing. Immersing myself in the memory of that moment, I realized my sadness was actually *grief*. How could that be?

For nine months, my husband and I had nurtured this baby without knowing its gender. I had imagined myself holding and dressing newborn Adam one minute and baby Emily the next and both felt real. As I wrote, the grief returned and its source became clear. With the arrival of Emily, there would never be an Adam. The loss *wasn't* real, but it *felt* real, and grief doesn't require rationalization. Writing my way through a contradiction recovered an experience and truth I'd lost.

Now Emily is the 17-year-old daughter whose laundry I fold unnecessarily, whom I look for when I hear footsteps on the porch, who will be leaving home to go to college in a few weeks. I experience sadness again for a loss that feels real but perhaps isn't. On the wall by her bed, there is a poster quoting legendary runner Steve Prefontaine. It admonishes, "To do less than your best is to sacrifice the gift." I think that applies to writing and parenting as well.

"Emily," I call out as she breezes through the foyer, always and forever on her way to someplace else. "Eat dinner at home before you go out. You'll be leaving a heartbeat from now."

"Mom," she says, with no desire to hurt me, "can't you see? I'm already gone."

"Get a dog," my friend Camilla advises when I recount with wistful acknowledgment my difficulty in letting go. "Get a dog like Harriet."

Harriet is Camilla's newest acquisition, a shelter dog, a tiny short-haired toy fox terrier mix that was possibly abused. When the dog was found, she was wearing pink nail polish, but only on one paw.

"That *is* abusive," I tell Camilla. "Who wouldn't run away?"

I want to point out that Camilla, too, has a 17-year-old daughter leaving for college in the fall. That maybe Harriet is compensation for Liz's leaving, but Camilla isn't buying it. "Here, Harriet!" she calls out and Harriet scuttles over. "Isn't she adorable?"

How do you find a story? Where do you find a subject? You show up at your desk with a well-intended and compassionate heart. Like someone at a dog shelter, you look over the possibilities and let the story find you. Feed it, nurture it, follow it.

Using What You Already Have

As *Washington Post* writer Joel Achenbach said when writing of evolution, "you can do almost anything with what you already have," but you must look closely. Like a water witch, a dowser, review your memories with your attention at the ready like a forked apple branch. You are a dowser of observation, of life experience, of the heart.

Look through scrapbooks and photo albums as if they can be decoded to reveal an insight. Who is always looking away from the camera? Who is behind the lens? What happened in the moments after the camera shutter froze the image? What was going on that particular day? At what point do you feel that tug on your attention that says "stop and dig here"?

Perhaps there's something about that photo of your eighth birthday dinner. Not who was crowded around the table, but the carrot cake your mother made that sat in the middle of it. The lumpy, homemade cake with its used candles from the year before (saved!) that she stayed up until midnight on a weeknight to bake for you. You loved that cake. She grated 3 cups of carrots for the batter. By hand. Nicked her knuckle. She made the cream cheese icing by hand as well.

You *should* have loved that cake. Only now you are a writer, which means you are plumbing beneath the surface for the truth. You are delving down through your emotions. What was it you were really feeling? You become curious, courageous, and willing to convict yourself if what you discover isn't commendable or particularly flattering. What is that nagging sense that something was off? What hasn't been quite in focus?

Unlike your parents, you didn't adhere to the philosophy that anything made by hand is better than anything mass-produced. Now you are looking at a picture of yourself blowing out those candles on your birthday cake. As an 8-year-old, you had been admiring the perfect fake confections from the supermarket your friends' mothers produced. Your mother could have bought one of those in five minutes, a perfect cake with symmetrical pink icing roses, your name in blue letters, and frosting as immaculate as first snow.

Why did everything have to be homemade? you had wondered. *Why did everything have to "Save!"?* *Were we poor?* And now, memory of your disappointment at her heroic efforts becomes your revelation. Did she guess how you felt? Were you good at hiding your feelings at the age of 8? Really? Where did you learn that? Are you good at it now? How could you have felt so loved and disappointed simultaneously; how could you have felt so *grateful* and disappointed at the same time?

Explore the contradictions and ask yourself questions. Scan your relatives for the person who affected you the least and consider the possibility that that person affected you the most. Make a list of three things you know beyond the shadow of a doubt—my mother loved me; my brother has more talent; I'm tenacious—and explore the idea that not one of these beliefs may be true.

I had a student whose parents never once told him he was loved, never once told him they were proud of his accomplishments, which were awesome by anyone's standards. Upon reflection, he realized he had never seen his genteel southern parents express affection to each other. Maybe the marriage had been an arrangement. Maybe they didn't love each other or him. Then he recalled one habitual gesture. After each meal, while his father read the paper and his mother had her tea, his father would raise his little finger where his hand lay on the table and his mother would hold it. That one picture of this cold, aristocratic man allowing his wife to hold just one finger was the type of paradoxical memory that could ignite an entire essay.

Another student, the daughter of missionaries, grew up on a Navajo Reservation. Her earliest recollection was of swinging from willow to willow, circling an entire meadow without touching the ground. She thought she'd grown up without the things that enriched other children's childhoods, yet she had never felt deprived. The source of abundance she'd felt in the face of poverty was identified as she shared her work with the class. Her earliest memory, it seemed, was of flying.

More Points of Entry

Think about a first or last experience—the first time you were kissed, hired, caught, promoted, embarrassed, experienced a miracle, woke up laughing, kept a secret, suffered a loss, made a mistake, were unjustly accused, had a nightmare.

Recall the last time you heard your name whispered, moved from a home you loved, saw something no one else saw, revealed a secret, passed judgment, were justly confronted, were envious. Review milestones, anniversaries, birthdays, promotions, graduations, weddings, births, but more personal milestones as well—the overcoming of a habit or fear—like learning to stop interrupting, learning to dive headfirst into a pool, learning to bridle a horse, learning to navigate a subway.

Write a memoir/essay based on a chronological listing of all your jobs or the evolution of your career; write of girlfriends, college roommates, homes, pets, or cars. Write of the cross-country road trip, the month with the Euro-rail pass, the mule ride to the bottom of the Grand Canyon. Why did you go, with whom?

Travel is the dominion of the muse. You are out of your comfort zone, in unfamiliar territory, so you are particularly receptive to new input. You go through intense periods of high-stress interaction, catching a train, boarding a plane, and then enforced periods of inaction, where you are left to ruminate, rocked on the railway track or gazing over the wing.

Write of the serendipitous incidents, the moment of panic where you thought you had boarded the wrong bus to Charles de Gaulle and were rescued by a 7-year-old boy who spoke English. Write of the people you met traveling and talked to for 20 minutes whom, surprisingly, you will never forget. The usual boundaries are more flexible—your seatmate may confide odd pieces of information, his history, hopes and dreams, because he knows subliminally you are a safe place to leave secrets. He is never going to see you again once the train reaches his station or the plane lands.

Traveling is a microcosm of life itself: you are on a journey with strangers, destination unknown, interdependent and connected. You will be leaving some people behind whether or not you are ready, you will be meeting others now destined to become your new companions on the adventure.

Great writing involves revelation—reaching for the unknown. Pontification is more useful behind a pulpit or podium.

Territory

Often students come to workshops after suffering the loss of someone they love. They don't come to learn to write, but to learn to live
again. For a while, grief is their turf. All of their exercises morph
into expressions of pain and loss. If this is you or someone you teach
or care about, try this: write about the loss for as long as you need
to. Write about the person, what you miss, how you feel. But at
some point, when you are ready, try writing *to* the person you are
missing instead of *about* them. Try writing a page describing something beautiful you saw on the way to work that you think they'd
appreciate, or something funny you overheard. Allow writing to
become a *conversation*, which implies by its very nature that you are
not really alone. Let writing be a bridge between pain and acceptance, acceptance and renewed well-being.

Most writers have a territory they explore for a time—perhaps an
entire career. It is the theme, subject, or question that predominates
their work. It might be a belief they hold—love triumphs over all,
everyone lies—and it might appear as a question, not an assertion.
In essence, they become specialists, like the artist Giorgio Morandi,
who painted the same collection of bottles and boxes in study after
study. This kind of revisiting makes possible a remarkable intensity
of observation, which in turn can elevate work to a higher plane.
What many writers find is that intense contemplation of a single
theme gives a freshness and individuality to each story even when
the subjects are similar. There is no shortage of writers whose work
can be described this way.

Amy Hempel once said that the territory of all her early stories
was loss and, indeed, her most famous short story, "In the Cemetery
Where Al Jolson is Buried," is about two college girlfriends, one of
whom is dying. Why select loss as a territory? Because as Hempel
makes clear, grief unites us.

John Cheever could be said to have written obsessively about suburban alcoholics. John Updike explored marital strife again and again. Alice Mattison once said that her territory changed after a decade of writing, and that at some point, writers tend to get done with a particular subject. It makes sense that after a thorough exploration a writer would set off for someplace new. Ask yourself whether you have a territory. What subject shows up in your work again and again? Is it time to break out? Is it possible you're done?

Sometimes a turf is a setting. Scott Russell Sanders writes about growing up near an army arsenal where old bombs were stored. He claimed his territory in his book, *The Paradise of Bombs*.

Sometimes the territory is a time, as it can be for historical novelists. Territory can be a form or an element that seems to show up in every story as well. The early works of John Irving, for example, seemed to invariably include wrestling.

Thinking about your work in terms of territory can give you a linking element in your short story or essay collection or allow you to recognize what a story you are struggling with is really about. I thought my territory was longing for many years. Then I looked more closely and saw that it was, in reality, abiding love.

Rocket Launchers

How else can stories and essays begin?

- With a list: "Here are the things I know by heart: the days of the week, the months of the year, all the state capitals ..."
- As a reflection: "I've always thought of myself as kind, but I am capable of ..."
- With reminiscence: "His name is 'Purfur,' my father said, pulling a small gray kitten from the inner pocket of his coat."

- With something you didn't know: "I thought Franny would never tell a lie."

- With a report of a past event or a crime: "Ten years ago a girl on her way to school doubled back through the woods to spend the day home alone."

- With a generality: "I've always believed suffering builds character …"

- With fascinating facts: "Everything in the universe is in motion, from the atoms that make up your coffee table, to the galaxies flying apart."

- With a portrait in words: "When I think of Alice, I see her as a girl so full of hope, it radiates from her body like heat."

- With a first or a last event: "My first day as a new mother I spent …"

- With an assertion: "No one under forty should get married." "No one is ready to become an orphan."

- With a conflict: "We always fought, but this time was different." "Too late," he says, "I've already started writing the ticket."

- In the middle of a discovery: "On January 10, 2002, I spotted a hole in the ice and my brother's hat lying near it."

- With a child narrator: "Nanna calls me Sugar Girl, but I'm only nice to Nanna because she gives me money."

- In the middle of an emergency: "The patient had been without oxygen for nearly two minutes."

- With a diagnosis: "'Will I become thin?' I wondered, looking at the incomprehensible nebula on the x-ray."

- With a mystery: "No one knows what happened to Alex."

Any one of these openings can be an essay or a story. They can begin in truth and become fiction; they can begin in fiction and contain truth. Inspire yourself by investigating other writers' points of entry. Take note of the opening sentences that stay with you, like the first sentence of Mark Richards's "Gentleman's Agreement": "The child had been warned." We're immediately hooked. Everyone has been a child. Everyone has been warned. A warning implies jeopardy. "*Had* been warned" raises the stakes. It implies the child didn't obey. You almost *have* to keep reading. Take a line like that and let it inspire one for your own use. "Perry was gonna get it," or "'He's got it coming to him,' Jackman thought as he approached the child."

There are an infinite number of ways to open a story. You have an infinite number of ideas to explore because you have a questioning and curious sensibility. As Mary Lee Settle says, "I start with a question. Then try to answer it." And Gordon Lish once observed that writers write to show how they solved the problem of being alive. We are all more alike than we are different. By expressing your fear, your disappointment, your triumphs, and your joy, you connect us all. What you wonder about, we all wonder about.

"If you're going to be a writer," says Louis L'Amour, "the first essential is just to write. Do not wait for an idea. Start writing something and the idea will come. You have to turn on the faucet before the water starts to flow."

4

The Science of Inspiration

"You can't wait for inspiration; you have to go after it with a club."
—Jack London

Paid by a program to foster the arts in public schools, Marta
Lowenstein taught dance after school every day at a New Haven
high school, almost always to girls. In college, twenty years earlier,
everything Marta did felt foolish and conspicuous. Then she took
a dance class, two more, and became serious. In large part it was
embarrassment—even humiliation—she became serious about. She
wasn't a natural and she was always being yelled at. She fell during
a performance. Worse, she wasn't hurt; she had to stand up, dance
some more, and bow. When she was alone that night, her shame was
mitigated by ambition: she would learn not to care. Marta is not easily
injured, and sure enough, after a while nothing troubled her. That is
how, of all her classmates, she became a dancer. The others wore out.

Alice Mattison opens "The Dance Teacher" with a character who
excelled in the arts through sheer tenacity. Writers need to be tenacious as well. Case in point: the poet William Stafford observed one
sure way around writers' block is to just lower your standards and
keep plugging away. And it's true that for most people it's easier to

improve work than to create it, especially when our personal critic (PC) is leaning over our shoulder with a red pen. But there are more enjoyable ways to inspire a writing career, and they have less to do with tenacity than biology.

If the PC is the internalized tenant you'd like to evict, the muse is the entity to which you'd like to rent the PC's room. Instead, there is this myth that the muse comes to town on a whim, might not drop by, never stays long, and leaves in the night with no forwarding address. It's a lot like trying to hail a cab in the sleet on New Year's Eve in Chicago. The muse is driving. You're wet and freezing. The cab's light says "Not in Service," and you think, *No kidding, I could see that coming,* but desperate, you step out into traffic and raise your arm anyway. You point, you signal, the cab nears, and you begin to wave wildly as if you are in third grade and are the only student in the row by the windows who can spell Mississippi. But the muse speeds on by, splashing you with cold water, and in your imagination, stops to pick up someone else. You feel panicked, helpless, left behind, and unable to do anything to be proactive.

But you *can* hail the muse and get him to stop. He's always available to serve you and you can absolutely facilitate inspiration, drawing it to you at will. Inspiration is subject to the same laws of biology and physics to which the rest of the universe responds.

Left Brain/Right Brain Facilitation

As mentioned in Chapter 1, brain lateralization plays an important role in accessing creativity. After decades of testing and research, it is now generally understood that the human brain is actually two brains—a left and a right hemisphere connected by millions of connecting nerve fibers (think switchboard) called the corpus callosum. While each half of your brain is capable of acting independently, each half has a specialty.

The right half of the brain retains and accepts the truth of any experience without requiring it to make sense. That is why it is the right brain that appreciates humor and understands metaphor. The right brain processes whole clusters of information simultaneously. It sees correspondences and resemblances, and recognizes faces when it cannot recall names. The right brain actually seeks patterns and looks for wholeness. It remembers complex images and is visual, evocative, and subjective. The right brain sees in pictures. It is intuitive. It is the source of inspiration and of emotional truths that defy logic.

The left half of the brain is in charge of sequential, linear processing. It recognizes fact and creates order. Your left brain engages every time you perform a routine task, such as sweeping a floor, taking a shower, or washing your hair, because it requires a linear sequence of events you do the same way every time: turn on the water, check the temperature, step in, wet your hair, uncap the shampoo, wash, rinse, and so on.

The left brain processes stimuli one at a time although at mind-boggling speed. It is verbal, understands syntax and mathematics, and knows how to place words together grammatically. The left brain controls your ability to write, so if you are writing an instruction manual, you'll be in great shape. However, unless you connect with the evocative right brain first, as a storyteller, you'll be stumped.

There is a direct correlation between physical action and inspiration. (There is a reason all those English poets walked the moors.) As Raymond Inmon confirms, "If you are seeking ideas, go out walking. Angels whisper to a man when he goes for a walk." It is not coincidence that ingenious story ideas seem to come while you are in the shower or great titles pop into your head while you're driving. This phenomenon, which is virtually universal, is the result of connecting with your right brain hemisphere by putting your left brain hemisphere into neutral through repetitive physical action—something you can do at will. As a writer you need to be able to access both halves of your brain, but it is the order in which you do so that invites inspiration.

It is as if your brain is actually a set of identical twins; they look the same, but the right brain is the artistic genius and the left brain is the analytical sister that prices her work and gets it to the gallery. They are so close, so used to working together, that they can complete each other's sentences, but as a writer, it is important to know the difference in personality and how to turn off the left brain with its need for logic when first sitting down to write. It is much as if you are inviting guests to a party but want the left brain to arrive late, after all the catching up between friends and connections between strangers have been established. In short, you don't want the left brain to show up until well after the dancing has begun.

Inspiration Becomes Habit

Our brains are constantly making new connections as we think new thoughts, and those new thoughts, if we think them often enough, physically change the structure of our brains. Neuron pathways that are used to read maps or memorize facts in medical or law school cause the hippocampus, seat of memory, to actually grow bigger. The more you write, the more you make it a habit to engage in connecting with your artistic right brain, the easier it will be to do so. You are creating an expectation of inspiration and forming a new habit.

Begin by believing you are creative whether or not you have fully demonstrated that fact in your life. Then begin to take small steps. You are retraining your brain to make associations, see patterns, think with originality, and put things together in a new way. Take drawing lessons like those originated by Betty Edwards in *Drawing on the Right Side of the Brain* and continued by her son, that accentuate *seeing* from the right brain. Like exercise, like dancing, the more you make a conscious choice to reach for original expression, the more natural it becomes. You are training a new muscle that will become stronger with use.

We have learned even more about the way our brains work as the result of some fascinating experiments done with patients whose brains were unable to communicate between the left and right hemispheres as a result of brain damage or surgeries. Researchers such as Dr. Michael Gazzaniga of the University of California have been able to show illustrations to just one half of a subject's brain at a time and then to ask the subject questions about what he has seen.

When the subject's left brain was shown something that didn't make sense or to explain a choice made by the right brain which, without access, the left brain could not comprehend, the subject—speaking from his left brain—would simply make something up. The left brain demonstrated it cannot tolerate anything but the logical to such an extent that it will glibly invent a fake past or scenario rather than live with an inconsistency. The left brain is on a constant vigil to make certain your inner and outer world reflect each other, whether or not that reflection is accurate. The left brain appears to be the seat of false memories.

It is as if the left brain arrives at the party in the most expensive dress and cannot accept the fact that the most expensive dress may not be the prettiest. It's just not logical. So the left brain will come to the "logical" conclusion that everyone at the party is blind. There, that explains it. The left brain cannot hold the tension of contradiction and yet the truth of our lives is often contained within that very inconsistency—in the events and experiences that don't make sense—in exploring the mysteries that will never be resolved.

Now that you understand the gifts offered by each half of your brain, you can tap into the skills specific to each hemisphere as desired.

Ways to Physically Trigger Inspiration

Since physical activity and habitual, repetitive movements like those associated with driving, running, walking, ironing, raking leaves, stirring soup, and showering all lull the left brain into neutral, you can purposefully schedule those kinds of activities before you sit down to write. They are equally helpful to do after a writing session. While the work is still fresh in your head, your brain will continue to make associations long after you have left your desk if you do not engage with other people but simply carry your thoughts with you into one of these kinds of activities. Remember, because those movements are sequential and repetitive, the left brain becomes engaged with them and will continue to allow the right brain to explore every image or seemingly unrelated thought that comes to mind.

This is why even doodling, drawing pictures or shapes while listening to someone speak, helps focus the mind. Psychologists are reporting that doodling is actually a memory enhancer. Keeping one hemisphere of the brain engaged in small motor movements allows that part of the brain to remain focused while the other takes in information and makes associations. That is why brainstorming works so well. Because your hand is literally circling words and darkening lines, the left brain is absorbed in those small, repetitive motor movements and the right brain is delighting in sudden insight, intuitive connections. Think about activities you do "on automatic" that will allow your right brain to drift and dream. Wash your car, split firewood, rock the baby, clean the gutters, fold the laundry, go for a walk, but keep a pen and paper nearby.

Tension as a Tool to Shift Hemispheres

It is not just the need for social contact that draws writers to cafés. It is another way to put the left brain into neutral. When you set up your computer in a coffee shop or anywhere there is the hum of life going on around you, the left brain gets engaged in filtering out the distractions and the right brain can go to the party without an escort. Try libraries, lobbies, airports, waiting rooms, and bookstores as well. Music can facilitate this connection, too, and many writers listen to particular favorites when writing.

There are many methods that will allow you to consciously neutralize left brain activity and invite inspired thought. As Alice Mattison notes:

> When I'm mildly stuck I wander around the house waiting for suppertime, because cutting up vegetables is helpful, or I walk my dog. Or I read poems. When I'm seriously stuck—whole days have passed—I look at art: paintings, prints, sculpture.
>
> What vegetables, poems, dogs and abstract art have in common is that they focus attention on what's not rational. A carrot does not think, it's just unapologetically there: orange, thick, pointed. And there's no talking the dog out of her honest pleasures, even the disgusting ones. Poets are as rational as fiction writers, but good poems don't arrive at a pre-ordained conclusion. Poems remind us to hear the sounds of words and the rhythm of sentences. They honor feeling, even when it's indefensible. The poems' surprises may shake us loose from predictable thinking.

At some point, however, you will want and need to make a left brain shift. Your left brain, when you are ready, will make sure that what you have written makes sense, that your words are in the right order, that your grammar is impeccable. Your job is simply to know which half of your brain you want to engage at any given time and to facilitate that connection.

Think of inspiration as a choice you make, not a request. Consciously choose to replace doubt with confidence, fear with faith. It feels weird at first, as if you are lying. "I have limitless ideas at my disposal" almost invites the left brain in to expose the charade. But

a belief ("I can't think of anything to write about") is just a thought
you've had for a long time—one you have charged with the emotion
of your doubt and fear. You've engrained it in your neural pathways
like a path through the snow. By consciously walking through the
drifts for a time, you will make new connections until the new path,
the one to easy creativity, becomes the one you choose.

Assume the muse is out there in a city cab, cruising the avenues,
looking for a fare. Step out and flag him down with kind and gentle
authority. When he stops to pick you up, just smile and tell him
where you want to go.

5

Navigating a Story

"How do I know what I think until I see what I say?"
—E. M. Forster

"Consider the hummingbird for a long moment. A hummingbird's heart beats ten times a second. A hummingbird's heart is the size of a pencil eraser. A hummingbird's heart is a lot of the hummingbird," observes Brian Doyle in his essay "Joyas Voladoras." Hummingbirds, Doyle tells us, visit a thousand flowers a day. They can fly 500 miles without stopping and dive at 60 miles an hour, but the price for such speed is more heart attacks and aneurysms than any other species on the planet. As Doyle observes, "It is expensive to fly."

What is this essay about? We don't know yet because good writing is like going on a trip without a map, and you often don't know your destination until you arrive. Which route to take, which side road to explore, will be a matter of instinct, intuition, and permission: the permission you give yourself to be surprised. Doyle goes on to contrast the tiny heart of the hummingbird with the heart of the blue whale, a powerhouse engine so massive it weighs more than 7 tons. Ultimately, this essay, born on the wing, is an observation about the human heart, its vulnerability, its fragility, and the inevitability that it will break.

The Gradual Progression Sensor

How does a writer discover that his true subject is the human condition when he began with observations about the hummingbird's heart? With a GPS: a Gradual Progression Sensor, which works a lot like your car's GPS.

My car's GPS has several choices for a voice, some of them male, but Jill's voice is the original and it feels rude to replace her. She does mispronounce a few things. For instance, "Spa Road" is "Sproad" in Jill-talk and she's not infallible. She doesn't know that new construction last year made a more direct route to Baltimore–Washington International available. My husband Clay needs to catch a flight that leaves in an hour, so while Jill makes suggestions I politely go my own way.

"Take Exit 21," Jill announces from the dashboard with good cheer, but as I approach the exit without slowing she becomes anxious, insistent. She emits a bonging noise to get my attention. "*Exit 21!* Turn right!" On the GPS screen the graphic representation of my car leaves the purple path Jill has plotted. There is a pause while she broods over this injustice.

"Re*cal*culating," she finally says in a somewhat nasal drawl.

"Jill's voice has a nasty edge to it, doesn't it?" I ask Clay.

He mulls this over. "I think it's more disappointed."

My family is scattered throughout the world—a son in New Zealand, a daughter in England, another daughter out of state, and a husband whose career often involves travel to another hemisphere. Like this morning, I am often on my way to an international departure lane at Dulles, Reagan, or BWI, but as I imagine the empty house to which I'll return, I wonder at this contradiction: Why is it that the people I love leave more often than they arrive?

This is how essays and novels begin; in a moment of observation—those hummingbirds! Those whales! Or, as we've said about contradictions, in a moment of curiosity about the illogical in your life. But then what?

Continuing the Story

On the way home, after I've left Clay at the curb of the United departures lane, Jill recovers but wants me to take Calvert Street home, which is fine but not the way I want to go. I actually hesitate, thinking I should take Calvert to please her. "I'm afraid if I defy her too many times, I'll scramble her brain," I tell Clay when he calls from the security line on Deck D. A baby squeals in the background cacophony of the airport.

"No you won't. She likes that. Take your own route."

And that is how writing continues—by following the energy, the intuition, the glimmer of interest in spite of the obvious and in defiance of the "shoulds." Never bypass an interesting side street no matter where you were headed. Your real destination is only this: where you arrive.

So don't worry if you frequently feel lost even in familiar territory. As Tezcatillipoca is often quoted: "You must travel at random, like the first Mayans. You must risk getting lost in the thickets, but that is the only way to make art." The trial and error method of finding your way through a story should be embraced. You may only know the route your story is going to take as far as the main character's next action, and you may need to recalculate constantly to accommodate each new idea.

In essay and story, you often have to feel your way home. Outlines and premises are great for term papers, but if *you* know where you are going in a creative piece of writing, chances are your readers know as well. Nothing is quite as disappointing as predictability nor as lovely as surprise.

"Explore spirit in terms of matter, matter in terms of spirit," Robert Frost said. If there is a feeling you want to explore, you begin in the concrete world. You describe real things, real circumstances, and let the spirit of the story come to it as mysteriously as the soul enters a child in the womb or as an idea becomes an invention. If you have only an event to describe, again, stay concrete and describe it, knowing spirit will materialize.

Imagine Frost in the dappled, quiet beauty of the Vermont woods. He comes to a fork and has a choice to make about which way to go. Perhaps later, in his study, Frost decides he wants to write a poem about choices and their ramifications in our lives, looks around for a metaphor, and writes "The Road Not Taken," but I suspect he was simply reliving a moment in the woods in all its physical perfection. As he described standing there, looking at the trees and the ground before him, he rendered matter on the page. The spirit of the poem was called into existence, becoming what it was about.

Let the Big Dog Hunt

One Christmas my husband and I bought an ant farm for our daughter Emily, then 5. It was briefly consuming, the ants fascinating as they made their tunnels one grain of sand at a time. The ant farm hovered in my mind as an oddity, a curiosity even, as I moved it from counter to table top and eventually up to Emily's room.

One day I decided the ant farm would be my point of entry for my writing time. "After Brian moved out, I bought our daughter, Erica, an ant farm," I began. "I thought it would distract her." I added an older adolescent brother, disproportionately angry and acting out, and came back to the ant farm, now describing the colony that inhabited it.

While Erica watches the ants exploring their new environment, I read little-known ant facts from the booklet that came with the farm.

Fact: Every worker has a full-time job to help everyone else in the colony.

Fact: All the workers are female.

Fact: A new colony begins with the marriage flight. Females and males mate in the air and then land. Afterward, the female scrapes off her wings and enters the nest forever.

It was just that—just an object, a description, no plan, no outline—but suddenly, a story began to emerge because that ant colony reflected the way the narrator felt about her life. Simply writing facts about ants exposed the plot and the metaphor. It was a route to take, a side road to explore.

You must trust this process. You are not seeking your subject. You are making yourself available for its arrival and once it does, your only job is to ask, "What happens next?"

The story you thought was about the girl with her ant farm is instead beginning to be about her disillusioned mother and disenfranchised adolescent brother. So you stay with them, describing their reactions, their world, but you do know this: something has to happen because whether you are writing an essay or a story, beautiful, insightful writing in which nothing happens is like looking at photographs of scenery from someone else's vacation. *Where are the people, where's the action?* you wonder. *Didn't you guys do anything?*

In this case, the brother, Adam, causes an accident with one angry, impulsive response: slamming a door shut just as his little sister slips her small hand between the door and its frame. The results are devastating. As soon as it is written, it is clear that the mother in the story has done this as well. With one impulsive action, an affair the son has discovered, she has brought devastating damage to the family she loves. Her actions are the source of her son's anger. That's what links them. Now the next few miles in the story's journey have been illuminated and I can follow the energy to the story's end. In the aftermath of the accident, which resulted in an emergency trip to the hospital, the mother finds Adam in his room anguished, remorseful, and full of adolescent confusion.

> *He is lying in bed, his back to me. Hidden under the peaks and valleys of the rumpled covers, the glint of his blond hair is the only clue that an outlaw hides in these hills. I sit down on the edge of the bed, my weight causing him to roll slightly, involuntarily toward me. I am in shock at what he has almost cost his sister tonight, but I know he didn't mean to hurt her. Looking at him, I think the truth is that we never set out to hurt each other.*

This story could have ended here perhaps. Because that thought was indeed one experience that had emerged as the story evolved: as often as we cause each other pain, virtually no one consciously sets out to harm someone else. We are more likely to be guilty of selfishness, self-absorption, of not having a clue. But this story, whose plot turned on the past action of an affair, was still following each side road. It was not a story about a little girl's ant farm, the road it first explored, or about a marriage, the first detour. It was a story about a mother and son, about regret and betrayal. It had become a story about disillusionment and abiding love. That was the destination that had manifested in the telling. That was the situation that required a resolution in the end.

> *I don't know what to say or do. I put a hand on Adam's shoulder but he doesn't turn. We sit in silence, the early spring moon rising like a life in its ascendancy, just outside his window.*
>
> *I lean down then, and awkwardly scoop the upper half of my son's body into my arms. He is dense—far heavier, I think, than a girl of similar age. I begin to rock him in the half light as I did in his infancy, and we both watch the moon, which appeared so near, rising higher through the trees. It becomes smaller, brighter; more intense as it gains distance.*

Suddenly he sags, as if whatever was holding him together and us apart has given way. He is now even heavier in my arms, and I imagine carrying him through blizzards or war zones. I pull him closer and do not speak.

You are your own Gradual Progression Sensor, a moment-by-moment navigation system. You sit down to write and ask yourself, "Where to?" but the image, event, or circumstance that comes to you is only your point of entry, a direction. "Where to?" is just the place where you get on the road.

The scenic route may not necessarily be the shortest distance between your location and your destination, but take each diversion and be receptive to whatever you find.

Start with anything (an ant farm or a hummingbird), trust the process, and let your story find its way. In the words of Barbara Kingsolver: "Don't try to figure out what other people want to hear from you; figure out what you have to say."

Part 2
Skills of the Craft

6

Teaching a Crow
to Talk: Voice

*"You do not create a style. You work, and develop yourself; your style is an
emanation from your own being."*
—Katherine Anne Porter

*I am not one to give a lot of advice but listen to me this one time.
Never, never, ever marry a woman named Trudy. No matter if she
is rich, beautiful or pregnant, don't do it. You will live to regret it
with every waking breath and in every nightmare. Trudy, Gertrude,
Gerty ... they hate the name. They hate writing it, listening to it
and no matter how it is said; it can never be said sexily. Men who
are married to Trudys are doomed to live forever because every day is
like a year.*

*Trust me. Believe me. It is one of my only three basic rules of
survival in this harsh world. The other two—don't pick your dentist
from an advertising sign on a bench and never trust a person who
tells you to trust him.*

Short story writer Paul Beckman has a recognizable voice. Whether
he is describing his family and its members' predilection for not
speaking to each other for years at a time or he's inhabiting a
character with the voice in "Showbiz," the preceding excerpt, his
is the voice of the personal adviser. As such, he is, in the guise of a

character, almost always telling the reader what to do. Beckman's narrator's voice is the bossy aunt or uncle who has just stopped by with some words of wisdom to improve your life. Guaranteed. Trust him.

Demystifying Voice

Hand in hand with subject, voice is the most important expression of yourself you can discover as a writer. Voice means your style. In essay, when you write authentically—without any attempt to speak as someone you are not—you are writing in your voice. Your voice is simply the voice in which you tell your story, in which you express your thoughts. In fiction, it is the tone, syntax, verb tense, rhythm, mood, and vocabulary used by the person narrating the action. Your authorial voice is the voice in your head. How can you discover your voice or refine it?

Try writing a letter to someone you trust, someone who understands you, gets your jokes, or shares a similar sensibility; someone who *likes* you. That person can be living or dead, the point being that you will speak or write to someone you trust in your natural voice. No pretensions, no artifice. When you are finished telling your story to this person, just cut off the salutation and closing and see what you have.

Connect with your voice by answering a compelling question such as "What breaks my heart?" "What do I find myself wanting most intensely for those I love?" "What is worse than betraying a friend?" Digging deeply into what you feel connects you to your genuine voice.

It is fascinating what happens to voice when the author is writing in a second language. Errors in grammar and an absolute ignorance of cliché can be remarkable and inspiring gifts of expression.

Chang Liu, a student in the United States from China, writes of the exquisitely painful moment in which he has to leave his girlfriend behind. He re-creates the scene where they stand under a bright porch light, forced by circumstances to say goodbye. The moment is so intense Liu becomes both participant and observer. "Her words keep on floating and I can hardly catch them down." Later he recaptures the experience in which he first stepped out into an American morning on his small-town college campus. It was the morning after 30 hours of flight, 12 hours of jetlag, and a life spent in the city "so long and monotonous I had become blind to nature."

> *The smell of the lawn sneaked into my nose. It tasted vibrantly green—for the first time I knew how to define what green is.*

And later,

> *I went for a morning walk along the stone path across the lawn. There were pearls of dew dancing gleamingly, weeds taller than me weaving a song according to the conduct of the breeze, and wild ducks floating on the creek at their leisure.*

Explore as many different voices as you can in order to identify your own. An easy way to expose yourself to a variety of voices at a glance is to review an anthology such as *Best American Short Stories*, *Best Southern Writing*, or *Best Science Writing*. By reading only the first few lines or paragraphs of each entry, you experience many styles in rapid succession, and the contrast helps you identify the voice you hear in your head. Sometimes you discover a voice that already sounds so much like you that it feels as if you have come home, found a relative, rediscovered your tribe.

I was living in New Zealand and excruciatingly homesick when I was invited to a formal reception in a private garden. New Zealand being part of the British Commonwealth, and the party being hosted by the prime minister, I was told that a certain decorum would be expected, and that the women would most likely wear dresses and hats out of tradition and respect. I went shopping in search of something I could wear on my head and was given a quick lesson on how a hat should be worn (a little cocked, like a beret, as opposed to straight on, like a cowboy).

If you had asked me what I was most homesick for living in temperate-zone perfection, I would have told you I missed days of sweltering heat, cars with steering wheels on the left, the utter extravagance of variety Americans enjoy in everything from ethnicity to brands of toothpaste. I would have said, "my friends, my home." I would probably not have said, "language."

The afternoon of the party, I entered the garden carrying my hat, which was the best I could do and still recognize myself. It was a lovely little accessory softened with a touch of creamy netting and grosgrain ribbon, but I felt like an imposter every time I put it on. Slender glasses of champagne bobbed on silver trays as waiters drifted through the crowd. I wandered through the party-goers as well, listening to the babble of accents around me. Everyone in New Zealand spoke English, of course, but with such thick accents and so much slang, I often was a bit lost at sea. (Mosquitoes were "mozzies," cookies were "biscuits," diapers were "nappies," the university was "unie.") My language, but not my language—like a cousin is not your sister.

There, beneath the dappled sunlight and surrounded by beds of purple agapanthus, brief snatches of conversation rippled and bubbled around me. The sound of human voices when you are lonely is like music. Gradually, I became aware of brief snatches of an American accent. I moved toward the sound as if to a homing beacon. I didn't know until that moment how much you can miss simply hearing someone else who speaks with the cadence, the emphasis, of the way *your* people speak the mother tongue.

When I got close enough, I could not only hear but *see* that the speaker was American. Of the hundreds of women around us, only she, too, was holding her hat.

Discovering your writer's voice is almost always accompanied by a sense of recognition, satisfaction, and completion. Like discovering among a crowd of strangers a lifelong friend.

Age of Innocence: the Child's Voice

Child narrators are distinctive and have many variations, such as the famously familiar adolescent voices of J. D. Salinger's *Catcher in the Rye*, and more recently, Mark Haddon's *The Curious Incident of the Dog in the Nighttime*.

To write in a child's voice means connecting with the child you were, with what was on your mind, with what a child would report:

My father says that you can teach a crow to talk. He is full of such lore. He says everyone should carry a pocket knife—even a girl. My father says when he was a boy, his dog was hit by a car but waited until my father got home from school to die. My father says he is leaving us, but I can visit.

My mother says she was born with second sight which she didn't need to see this coming. She says never to ask for candy at someone else's house and that anything you want to know, you can find out at the library.

My sister says that when I was born she had asked for a horse and my parents asked for a boy. She says I'm going to marry Sir Peesalot and that I should name my doll Mucous.

My father says the spirit was willing but the flesh was weak. My mother says we are what we do, not what we say. My sister says if only you'd been a boy.

If you find memory to be a good launch pad or more inspiring than imagination, you may find that the voice of a child narrator is a good fit. Be forewarned, however, that the virtues of this voice are its vices as well.

Child narrators can be quite young, such as the distinctive voice in Kay Gibbon's *Ellen Foster* or the 5-year-old Jack in Emma Donoghue's *ROOM*, or Burt in Howard Buten's novel *When I Was Five I Killed Myself*. Many child narrators, however, end up being around the age of 12 because the age gives you enough latitude to have some fairly astute observations. The advantage to writing as a child is that preaching and pontificating are almost impossible. It is a voice that forces you to show more than you tell, and every tool you can use to enhance this skill is desirable.

The disadvantage is that you must stay consistent. You must never allow your narrator to draw conclusions or have insights beyond his years. Your vocabulary must ring true, and sometimes this is limiting. You must also have an excellent memory—not only for the syntax of the way a child speaks, but an awareness of how and what a child sees and feels. When a child of grammar school age enters a doctor's exam room, what he sees (needles!) from his physical height (needles!) and notices from his mental focus (needles! needles! needles!) is different from what an adult sees. What he would be curious about and choose to comment on would be different as well. Your job is to maintain authenticity on every level.

The Unreliable Voice

A child narrator can be reliable—your child narrator can be the only person telling the truth in your story or essay—or a child narrator can be *un*reliable, telling the reader what happened but obviously drawing the wrong conclusion. This adds resonance to voice (adult or child) as doubt about whether to trust the narrator echoes in the reader's mind.

Sometimes the reader doesn't know for quite a while whether or not the narrator is even sane, and that tension is a wonderful mystery that keeps your reader turning pages. In this example, from "Not Wisely, But Too Well," George Sherblom reels us in tighter and tighter with an adult narrator whose reliability is immediately in question.

This is not stalking. I am not a stalker. It's true that she doesn't know me; but I am doing nothing wrong. Truly, if I am anything, I am her protector.

I am not hiding. I have just arranged my position to reduce the likelihood that I will be noticed. Someone looking for me would have no trouble seeing where I am. I am merely not drawing attention to myself.

I am not a threat to her. This I can swear. I have no desire to interfere with her life. I will not touch her, speak to her, even approach her. I just want to observe her, admire her, appreciate her.

And so I watch and wait. It is late May. I will keep checking through the first few weeks of June. Sometime during this period, biology demands that she climb out of the pond and lumber towards some sandy place of her choosing. There she will lay this year's eggs and perhaps add to the pond's population of snapping turtles.

The unreliability of a narrator can also be purposely funny and without any tension at all, as in Paul Beckman's story, "Gospel."

Her name is Letitia and she lives in the City New York. She teaches creative writing at Columbia and writes stories for Cosmo, Redbook *and the like. She will make me the villain in one of her stories. Remember. I am not the villain.*

Don't believe everything that you read.

I live in the suburbs of Connecticut and got her name through friends of friends and called her one Sunday evening. My story is gospel. She will write that I answered her ad in the Village Voice *Personals. That will be a lie also. I don't even read the personals. Ask anyone who knows me. I'm not the kind of guy who would or could do such a thing. Besides, I don't know what all those*

abbreviations stand for, and no one ever tells the truth in those ads.
You don't know what kind of person you will wind up with.

Now compare that character's voice analyzing a woman's romantic motives with the eloquent, reserved, but intimate voice of Wallace Stegner in *Angle of Repose* and you'll see just how different two voices can be:

> *I don't think she was protecting herself from an attachment she feared*
> *might leave her on the bough. I don't think there was that much of*
> *an attachment, not on her part. He kept writing, and she didn't have*
> *the heart to shut him off. And he was a reserve possibility, a hole card*
> *that she didn't look at because she didn't want to risk breaking up the*
> *beautiful sequence of hearts face-up in her hand.*

Other Universal Voices

The reminiscent voice, in which the narrator is looking back, remembering the past, is another universal style, and while it is the obvious choice for a memoir, it is just as appealing when used in fiction.

"In the years after we first moved to the shores of the Hazel River, it continued to freeze over in winter, a thin glaze that rendered a mirrored moon." And remember you are not limited to writing in any one particular person. For example, try a reminiscent voice in third person: "The Elliots had owned Hawk's Hill for five generations. Only Mark Elliot knew ghosts were among its occupants."

The action voice is another style with universal appeal. This style tends to be abrupt, intense, to the point with more short sentences, more dialogue. Like the reminiscent voice it, too, is a compelling vehicle for writing in any person: first, second, or third.

First person action: "Jack bolted, but they caught me cold." Second person: "You know you're in trouble when you've talked in your sleep." Or third: "John shouted. Only the moon heard him and she did not respond."

What feels natural to you? Is your preferred voice casual and conversational? Formal? Does the voice in your head speak with a British accent? A Southern dialect? Is it a voice that relies heavily on dialogue? Or does your inner narrator tell a lot of back story and history, like someone telling a story to a child at bedtime? Is it a snappy voice that rivets the reader or a melodic voice that mesmerizes?

Maybe you find the intimate voice of a diarist appealing, the confessor of secrets. Maybe the detached, dry commentator voice of a reporter is more your style. Perhaps you would like to use a dispassionate voice to write of something very emotional. You could use a strictly factual voice for instance and let the reader make the right brain leap to your real subject, which could even be humorous.

Suppose you picked up an essay that began: "The male New Zealand kakapo, almost extinct, sends a booming mating call to females all night in order to attract a mate. Unfortunately, he normally attracts predators which eat him first." Now imagine the title is "Why I Don't Date" or "The Hazards of Karaoke and Other Mating Rituals." Maybe yours is a memoirist's voice, or an historian's, a chronicler's, a correspondent's, a scientist's. Try them all and experiment with each in first, second, and third person.

Verb tense is an important element of shaping a voice. Try a narrative voice that speaks in the present and then try switching to past tense. For example: "My brother Charles is calling. I can tell by the insistent, aggressive ring of the phone." Or "My brother Charles called. I knew by the insistent, aggressive ring of the phone." Present tense is immediate and sometimes less difficult for a new writer because you are held in the moment and less likely to go off on tangents, but don't limit yourself to writing in one verb tense or one voice alone. Mix them up. For example, present tense is just as effective in third person: "Mary searches the beach for her daughter's footprints. She avoids the water's edge and turns toward the dunes."

Most writers become comfortable with writing in one particular tense or person. In so doing, they develop a somewhat recognizable narrative voice. No one would mistake the long, flowing sentences of Faulkner with the pragmatic, often repetitive style typical of Hemingway. And the utter poetry of Ron Hansen's voice comes through every novel. In *Atticus* he writes: "Weeds and sage were yellow against the snow and the snow strayed over the geography as though recalling how it was to be water." Some versatile writers pick up a new voice in each work, such as Geraldine Brooks (*March, Nine Parts of Desire, Year of Wonders*). Tim O'Brien is adept at this as well. Compare the voices in "The Things They Carried" and *Tomcat in Love*.

A Duet: Combining Voices

You can also combine voices to great effect. Take the dry, factual, and heavily researched voice of George Sherblom in his essay "Wakened." George had been in a bicycle accident and was knocked unconscious when he hit a pothole and flew headfirst over the handlebars. In his painstaking account of coming back to consciousness, he recounts how alert nurses can break up the tedium of a long shift with a bit of sport at the expense of their patients. George's voice remains factual, which only accentuates the effect of his "footnote."

> ... *The recovery room nurses must be alert to any flickering movement on their charge's face if they are to ask the patient if he knows where he is before he can possibly provide a cogent response. Once, as I emerged from anesthesia, I heard the staff's vigilance pay off handsomely. Another patient—when addressed by a nurse before he could clear his head—asked for his "birth-control glasses[1]."*

> 1. I must also observe that, ever since, I have been intrigued with the notion of birth-control glasses, something that so worsens the appearance of others that the idea of mating and reproducing with them becomes abhorrent. I can see fathers responding to their daughters' requests to go out

for the evening, saying, "You must be back by 11, and wear your birth-control glasses the whole time."

Experiment

To find your voice, experiment. National Public Radio ran a phenomenally popular program for many years called, "This I Believe." Listeners were asked to write exactly 500 words on something they felt was true. It could be a testament on absolutely any subject; the only requirement was a passionate conviction that the writer was espousing a truth. They could be persuasive or simply a reminiscence. A writer could believe in love at first sight or UFOs. He could tell a story that culminated in his belief, "my dog has a soul," or start right out with an assertion: "men are never on time." The only rule was that at someplace within those 500 words, the phrase "this I believe" had to appear—the writer had to make a stand. The station was flooded with responses. They archived them online. People who thought they were not writers wrote hilarious or thought-provoking essays. And they wrote in their own voices.

Why?

Because just as with writing a letter to someone with whom you feel safe, when you feel passionately about something or feel an intense need to make your point known, that urgency almost always causes you to speak in your authentic voice. There's no need to mimic others or look around. You have something to say and you are inspired by your conviction to say it. As Ray Bradbury says, "When was the last time you dared release a cherished prejudice so it slammed the page like a lightning bolt?"

So try it yourself. Take a stand. Claim your ground. If you are in doubt about your voice, ask yourself, "What do I believe?" Make a list. "I believe in keeping a promise, that the robins are bigger each spring, that first-born siblings are smarter, that my grandmother was clairvoyant, that midwesterners are friendlier than southerners, that cats are superior to dogs."

All great masters have had apprentices—from sculptors to musicians—and it is just as honorable a tradition for writers, even though you will most likely never meet the author of the work that mentors you. But if you discover a voice that speaks to you, imitate it as a means of inspiring yourself to write. You will refine your own voice over time. Write in a voice that is the voice you like to read, the voice you hear in your head. Just have a conversation on the page. Get the voice right, and everything will follow.

As Sarah Shun-Lien Bynum's narrator explains in *Ms. Hempel Chronicles:* It is seventh grade parents' night, and Beatrice Hempel wants her students' parents to understand why she chose to have the class read Tobias Wolff's *This Boy's Life.* The book has some questionable language in it and her choice has been challenged by a parent. Ms. Hempel picked it, she says, because it reminded her of *Catcher in the Rye* and the way the eighth graders respond to that book is always so amazing she wanted the seventh graders to have a similar experience.

> *Because every time I teach* Catcher *to the eighth grade, I feel like I'm witnessing the most astonishing thing. It's like they've stuck their finger in a socket and all their hair is standing on end. They're completely electrified. What they're responding to, I think, is the immediacy and authenticity of the narrator's voice. And part of what makes Holden sound authentic to them is the language he uses. This book's impact on them is just—immeasurable.*

One by one the parents start to admit their kids can't put the book down. "Well done!" says a father and the parents break into applause.

The power of voice has made lovers of literature out of kids who didn't even want to take English.

Ms. Hempel, standing at the front of the classroom, wanted to bow.

7

Talk to Me: Dialogue

"Words are, of course, the most powerful drug used by mankind."
—Rudyard Kipling

"Not many people know this," she said, "but there are four times as many fatalities from bee stings as from snake bites."

Noah couldn't bear to watch her give herself the injection. Crouching at the base of a pine tree beside the trail, he scanned the woods for bees, wasps, hornets. Suddenly the forest seemed a sinister place, full of small but deadly hazards.

"You'd better get me to a hospital," she said, returning the syringe to her first-aid kit. She was sitting against the tree, this woman he barely knew, her curly brown hair dangling to her shoulders. She looked healthy. She looked fine. His only experience with allergic reactions had been his mother's sniffling and sneezing every spring when pollen rode the air like a flock of microscopic geese.

"Cardiovascular collapse," she said, as though responding to a question from the jaybirds swooping down from the canopy.

Alan Elyshevitz opens his story "Noah's Ark" with dialogue and allows dialogue to carry the entire scene. The narrator, Noah, is on a date with a woman who is going into anaphylactic shock because she neglected to tell him she has a fatal allergy to bee stings before a hike in the woods. He has less than 60 minutes to carry her down a deserted mountain in the rain to seek emergency medical help and he doesn't even like her. Casting the scene in dialogue makes the action feel immediate, as if the reader is there watching the clumsy, urgent trek down the mountain.

> "Can't you just keep taking the shots until we get back?" he asked.

> She shook her head. "Each one lasts about fifteen minutes, but after an hour or so, the medication stops working."

> "How can you be so calm?" he asked her.

> "I'm not," she said, raising a hand to her heart.

> At his suggestion, she climbed on his back, and he hooked his wrists beneath her knees. It was only their second date, and this was the first time their bodies had touched ....

> "Ride high," he said. "As high as you can." ...

> "Annie told me you were more than muscles." Her lips were close to his ear, as though they were talking in bed. "She said you were a real sweet guy."

> "I don't know about that."

> "Who else would carry me to safety?"

> "Anybody."

Using Dialogue for Effect

Dialogue is a way of showing the nature of a relationship instead of explaining it. When Noah responds to his date's flirtatious question with the dry and accurate "Anybody," he lets the reader know how unromantic this situation is and the absurdity of the question. Struggling to carry this girl off the mountain is not a matter of affection, but duty.

In addition, by using the correct punctuation, it was possible for the author to omit speech identifiers. The uninterrupted flow creates an immediacy that continues as the drama unfolds. Noah is still wrestling with his irritation as he works against the clock to get help.

There was a question on his mind, and he tried not to sound accusatory when he asked it. "Why did you agree to go hiking with me … in your condition?"

"My condition?"

"I said it would be an all-day trip out in the middle of nowhere."

"You invited me."

"I didn't know about your problem with bees."

"I don't have a problem with bees."

Right, he thought. They have a problem with you.

When you do use identifiers, use the simplest form. It is hard to improve upon "said" and variety only distracts:

"I can't go with you," he moaned.

"You've got to be kidding," she replied.

"No, I'm not," he retorted.

"Then just leave!" she exclaimed.

Note as well that an exclamation point indicates an exclamation. It doesn't then have to be followed by the word "exclaimed."

Another way to use dialogue to create an effect is to leave out the quotation marks. The conversation becomes subtly more inclusive of the reader, as if the brackets embracing speech had been holding the action in and the reader out. Eliminating them subtly invites the reader into the intimacy of the story.

Contractions

Although dialogue is artificially crafted, it has to sound the way people talk. For instance, it would sound absurdly formal to say, "I cannot come to the movies tonight, so do not wait for me," unless this sentence was being uttered by a character for whom English is a second language. "I can't come, so don't wait." Contractions make stilted language sound genuine. It's a little like highlighting your hair: It takes a lot of artifice to make those blond streaks look natural.

Context

Bub, pal, buddy, dude—beginning writers often neglect to make dialogue unique to each character. In reality, a teenager will accuse someone of being "lame," "jazzed," "pumped," "stoked," a "flamer," "hot," or a "poser," whereas his parents might use the words "inadequate," "excited," "thrilled," "inspired," "jerk," "attractive," or "pretentious." Sex under the age of 30 is "hooking up," and kids don't get together, they "hang out" or just "hang." They say "sweet" in response to good news, and someone who has done something worth commenting on "rocks." They say "like" and "whatever" in response to almost everything. Case in point, I was once in a department store standing at a cosmetics counter near two teenage girls. The dialogue went something like this:

"Oh my gosh, like, you should've seen her! She was, like, crazy or something. She was like, yelling at me, I don't know, like she was nuts!"

A well-dressed older gentleman was looking at scarves nearby. It was obvious that he, too, could not help overhearing the conversation. He turned to the young speaker and said, "Are you aware of how often you repeat the word 'like'? All of you young people say 'like,' all the time. It's absurd! I'll bet you said 'like' ten times in the last two minutes."

The girl looked him in the eye and said, "Like who cares?"

So keep your dialogue distinct. Teenage characters use expressions older characters cannot even decode; by the time you read this, teenagers will be speaking in yet a new code, so be careful about dating your stories with language. However, remember that a scene in a restaurant involving an old man, his middle-age daughter, and her adolescent son will have to reflect age-appropriate dialogue to have any authenticity.

"I'd appreciate it if you could just give us a minute please," the elderly gentleman said to the young waiter orbiting the table with pen and pad.

"For heaven's sake, back off," snapped his daughter, exasperated at being rushed.

"Dude! Like, back down," said her son.

Another aspect of context is to keep in mind that good dialogue is not just how characters speak but what they speak about. If my character directs and redirects the conversation to herself, I can show anxiety or narcissism without a label. If my character talks obsessively and negatively about a co-worker, I can show she is a gossip, or envious. Context is particularly important when children speak in your writing. The cadence of children is age-specific, as are the things they talk about.

In Lisa Shea's novel *Hula*, two young sisters are watching a thunderstorm approach from their front porch. Inside the house, their violent father shouts at their mother. The terse authenticity of Shea's dialogue is what makes the book so compelling.

My sister covers her ears. From behind a cloud rimmed in green, lightning flashes.

"Heat lightning," says my sister, too loud.

"It might be real lightning," I tell her when she puts her hands down.

"Real lightning can kill you," she says.

As the argument in the house escalates, their mother opens the door and tells the girls to get the dog and get in the car. They're going to have to escape to the safety of a friend's house for the night. The rain begins in earnest as the girls run for the car.

"This is the safest place in a lightning storm," my sister says. "Because of the tires."

"What about them?"

"Shut up," she tells me. "It's science."

New writers often forget that not every observation or accusation a character makes requires a rejoinder. No response is, in fact, a very telling response: let a comment or question reverberate in the air. This is especially effective when your characters are in conflict. Have your character walk out, look away, or pick up a glass, in lieu of a verbal retort. In the preceding scene, the girls wait in the car so long that the older sister, in the front seat, feigns sleep. But first, eyes closed, she orders her little sister not to look at her.

Instead of responding, the little sister reaches out from the backseat with one small hand and carefully grasps the tiniest end of her big sister's blond ponytail to which she hangs on, undetected and protected, as the storm rages.

Padding and Pacing

Dialogue has to convey character, be authentic in diction and tone, and not draw attention to itself any more than a new pair of shoes should distract from a great outfit. It should simply accessorize a great story. Dialogue also has to move your story along at an entertaining pace. To do so, it cannot afford any empty words or padding.

A telephone conversation is pure dialogue and on television, where every second of airtime can cost thousands of dollars, you can see economy of words in action. Rarely, if ever, does the conversation end with "goodbye." Phone conversations on television are more likely to end with phrases that contain action: "Make it happen," or "I'll take care of it," or "On my way." "Goodbye" is an empty word, a redundancy that would just slow the action.

Empty phrases in your dialogue also slow your story: "Well," "Look," "I don't know," "What?" "How come?" "Hmmm," "Huh?" and "I guess" are common examples. Try cutting all of these from your dialogue and you'll find those trimmed scenes move along at a more compelling tempo. Be it slow or fast, skillful pacing is vital to a well-told story. In "Noah's Ark," the author purposefully slows the conversation to show the girl is nearing death. She stops initiating speech, then stops responding to speech, then stops making any noise at all.

She made a guttural sound he could not interpret. When she tried to swallow, she coughed into his ear. Her lungs whistled. Little by little she slipped down to his waist, and no matter how often he stopped to boost her higher on his shoulders, she always sagged back down again.

When it was time for her next dose of medication, Noah eased her down beneath the inadequate shelter of a leafy birch. Her eyes were open and she was breathing, but she couldn't speak.

But in Paul Beckman's "Come! Meet My Family!" the dialogue is fast and intense. It carries the entire piece and the pace adds pressure. The reader only has access to what one person is saying and must intuit the other character's response.

You! Don't worry. They are going to love you. Just be yourself!
Don't gush. Sometimes you gush. They hate gush. I think it's
adorable personally. No. Never be obsequious—worse than gush.
This is not like an inspection, it's a simple meeting. Don't worry.
If I love you, they will love you. Guaranteed! Don't wring your
hands, they will take it as a sign of weakness. No—blasé is no
good, inquisitive is O.K. if it's not like nosy, not indifferent, nor too
well dressed or attractive (that's high falutin). Not sloppy, they hate
sloppy. Just be yourself. Don't hang on me. Of course I like it! They
will say clingy. Don't stay away. Remote and uncaring—I can hear
it now. Stop worrying.

To write effective dialogue, you must listen to the conversations around you. Tune your ear, pay attention, and take notes. After you get it down on the page, revise and cut. Treat the writing of dialogue as if you were writing a poem—make it precise and well crafted, with an emotional takeaway that serves the scene. If you want to leave the reader with a sense of crisis, you can do that with dialogue. If you want to leave your reader with a smile, you can do that, too. This is a world in which you speak for everyone.

Ending with Dialogue

Opening a story or essay with dialogue is intense and immediate, but it's a powerful way to end a story as well. Let the character's words resonate in the reader's mind, keeping him present until the last page.

In Linda Woolford's story "The Space Between," teenage Sylvie's younger brother Sam is dying of leukemia. Sylvie has been taking drawing lessons as a distraction, learning about negative space. Space comes to an end then goes on forever, Sylvie is told. Space is deep but never empty, she learns. Looking at the sky through the spaces between her fingers, Sylvie sees branches, then the space

between the branches; leaves, then the space between the leaves.
"The sky like bits of mosaic, the dark branches like the lead of
stained glass." Wanting to share her evolving perspective of what
constitutes reality, what is real, and what will last, she comes to
Sam's sickroom after class.

*"Want to come up?" he asked, shyly. I climbed onto the bed and
felt his feather weight against me. I opened the portfolio and began
to spread the drawings. I held one up.*

"Look at that space," I said. "Do you see? You can draw it."

*His eyes were enormous, glassy, as he traced the shape between
the torso and the candelabra. "It's like monsters," he said. "I see
monsters." Startled, I followed his finger as it moved through my
drawing. I felt I was tumbling, what I knew of the world shifting,
as he continued to outline the shapes of space I'd drawn. They rose
menacingly from the paper.*

*"Cool," Sam whispered. "How did you learn to do that?" He
looked at me with surprise. "Can you show me? Come on, Sylvie."*

*I looked at the drawings. At my brother. He was disappearing.
Soon I would be able to see through him. There was nothing now
that I could show him. I picked up his hand. It was light as a leaf,
the lines in his palm red. He would show me.*

*"Stretch your fingers as wide as you can and look at the space
between," I said. "Tell me what you see."*

8

Quintessential Elements

"I would never write about someone who is not at the end of his rope."
—Stanley Elkin

Lucky is a rotund, rugby-ball shaped mutt with a glass eye, a steel hip and marbled wispy fur coming through in sparse mangy patches. He has been hit by three cars and nearly killed twice and still chases any wheeled vehicle without hesitation; it's his job. He is still wearing a superman cape Caroline put on him last year; he loves it and it adds to his mystique. He comes and goes for weeks at a time, and is hopelessly in love with Beauregard but the cat is wholly unimpressed. Caroline tries to bathe him but Lucky is gross even for her overly sympathetic temperament and she never lets him inside.

Lucky rearranges himself on my chest, his front paws on my shoulders, his maniacal grin and oversized tongue unrolled out the side of his panting mouth, inches from my face. He's so ugly it's poetic; it's his smell I can't abide.

—A. C. Oliver, *A Southern Introduction*

Quintessence refers to the purest possible embodiment of a characteristic or a trait. Lucky, for example, is not just unappealing—he's ghastly, repulsive, a quintessentially ugly dog. We love quintessential elements because we are fascinated by extremes. They are staples of both classic and modern literature. When animals are the subject of stories, they almost always embody quintessential traits. Secretariat was the fastest horse; Black Beauty, the most long-suffering; and Moby Dick was the greatest whale.

The literature of childhood is full of quintessential elements. Rapunzel's hair. The sword Excalibur. Or how about the two sisters in "The Fairy's Mistake," one so quintessentially good that when she spoke, pearls and rubies fell from her lips, while her sister spewed bugs and snakes?

Whatever you want to portray—beauty, kindness, danger, fear, strength, violence—take it to the max. We don't want a runaway train; we want a runaway train with a deadly toxin on board, without a conductor, barreling toward a village full of sleeping children. We don't want a wave; we want a tidal wave caused by an asteroid. We don't want rich; we want super-rich. *Über*-rich. Not just intelligence, but genius. And give us Dr. Evil, not your everyday dictator. Think about it. Which is more intriguing: a murder, or a perfect murder?

We read about ordinary people, but we're more interested if they're in extraordinary circumstances. Flannery O'Conner, in "A Good Man Is Hard to Find," demonstrates this when an ordinary family has a car accident on a remote stretch of road and is discovered by an escaped convict and his crazy accomplices.

The Misfit and his fellow sociopaths have no intention of helping this vulnerable family as each one is taken for a short "walk in the woods." The grandmother, terror distorting her reality, suddenly sees The Misfit as if he were her own child. She impulsively reaches out and touches him on the shoulder. The Misfit instinctively recoils as if bitten by a snake and shoots the old woman three times in the chest. Then he calmly lays the gun down in the dirt before taking off his glasses and cleaning them.

The Misfit is not just bad, he's super-bad, and that is what makes him so compelling.

The extraordinary circumstances can be quintessential without being a matter of life and death. Writer Jeanne Slawson worked in Egypt as a young woman and was invited to the home of a local man and his wife, Soahd, in return for helping the gentleman with some research. "My wife will cook many things," Mohammed said. Jeanne felt that eating everything she was served would be essential to international etiquette, and in so doing ate a quintessential meal.

My plate is filled—one very large piece of chicken with runny green sauce, one peak of a vegetable mountain, green, orange and yellow, two red potatoes stuffed with meat. In the powder room I unbutton my waistband. I'm just able to finish my meal. When Mohammed offers seconds I decline politely. "But we eat and then we renew!" he says. "In our country guests do not stop eating until their hosts do."

I accept another chicken breast with green lava, more vegetables, another potato. More food is offered but I am cheerfully firm in my refusal.

"But we eat and then we renew!"

Finally they push their plates away. I have consumed two and a half green chicken breasts, two pounds of vegetables and five meat-stuffed potatoes. Soahd has fetched homemade baklava and gives two to each of us. I'm finishing the largest individual meal in history but no! She's bringing something else!

We also like reading about extraordinary people trying to lead ordinary lives (the game-theory genius played by Russell Crowe in *A Beautiful Mind* or the savant played by Dustin Hoffman in *Rain Man*). What you are not likely to read is a story about someone ordinary doing something mundane. In other words, you will never read a story about most people. Why would anyone read that story when they can look in a mirror? Instead, we love entering a world where we get to live out things that are not likely to happen to us. We probably won't discover we're the heirs to a billionaire's fortune or that we carry a mutation that allows us to fly, but we like to read about people who do.

Any story element can become quintessential. Start with a character such as James Bond. He's the embodiment of debonair sophistication, resourcefulness, skill, and romantic appeal. He's enabled in his quintessence by quintessential gadgets. His car can be driven on water, fly, fire missiles, or eject its driver if necessary. His pen is a camera and a weapon. His shoes explode.

Or how about Lisbeth Salander, the heroine of Stieg Larsson's *The Girl with the Dragon Tattoo*? She's the quintessential computer hacker. She's not just good at it; there's virtually no system she can't breach in a matter of minutes. She also embodies more than one quintessential trait. She is the extreme social misfit, unable to participate in a world of social conventions, unable to love or be loved. Both quintessential qualities work together to advance the plot, and we love quintessential plots. (Why save the town when you can save the country? Why save the country when you can save the human race? Why save the human race when you can save the entire planet?) And we are fascinated by quintessential circumstances as well.

Neglect and poverty? For memoir, read Jeannette Walls's *The Glass Castle* or Frank McCourt's *Angela's Ashes*. For fiction, think John Steinbeck's *The Grapes of Wrath*.

So how do you keep a character or situation that is such a singularly perfect embodiment of a trait from becoming cartoonish? Maybe the quintessential trait is subtle, like tenacity, selflessness, fidelity, loyalty, or faith. Or give your quintessential character a flaw—a quintessential one. Show the reactions of those around your character, very real people who don't have any extra special talents but who love, fear, fail, and hope in the usual ways—in humanity's ways.

The world's best medical diagnostician, Dr. Gregory House, is addicted to pain killers, a weakness that shows his damage as those around him try to deal with both quintessential talent and its accompanying weakness. Quintessential hero Superman was vulnerable to kryptonite. Achilles' mother would have made him immortal when she immersed him in the River Styx if the poor woman hadn't forgotten to re-dunk him to include his heel—now the quintessential symbol of anyone's place of vulnerability.

In addition to characters, settings can be quintessential: set an ordinary story on an asteroid, or on a speeding bus with a bomb beneath it, or in an insane asylum, or on Antarctica, and it becomes an entirely different tale. Make the story take place climbing Mt. Everest, in the Sahara, or in the most remote village in the rain forest. Perhaps your setting is the harshest boarding school in England or the most crime-ridden city in Mexico. Maybe it takes place in a version of Camelot or Shangri-La.

Quintessential characters and settings eventually become code for the quality they embody. "He's a Don Juan" and "He's a real Sherlock Holmes" mean "He's a playboy" and "He's brilliant at reasoning." And real people can become part of our lexicon as well. "He's a real Fred Astaire." "He's a real Houdini." "She's a Mother Teresa." "He's an Einstein." *The Perfect Storm*, originally a book, now is an expression meaning a rare combination of disastrous circumstances. Other settings have also gone on to become code: The Alamo, Eden, and Waterloo.

We began looking at quintessential traits with the ugliest dog of all time; we should contrast Lucky with Lassie, who was, perhaps, the most clever.

Lassie could communicate in English like a canine telepath: "Hello, Timmy. The barn is ablaze but I've saved all the horses." Of course, comedian Dave Barry points out, it may not have been that Lassie was quintessentially smart as much as it was the fact she was owned by (quintessential) idiots. How could these people remain clueless week after week when Lassie appeared on the scene barking wildly to get their attention, ran off in the direction of *smoke*, looked pointedly back, and barked again?

"Whadda ya want, Lassie-girl? Heh-heh, look! Lassie wants to play!" Whatever the true quintessential trait, the stories made great entertainment.

Of course the world is full of quiet stories of gentle insight. They enrich our lives and feed our souls, but they rarely come out at the box office. If they do, magnificent or not, it's an indie film with limited distribution, like *The Parrots of Telegraph Hill*. Next time you sit down to write, think about creating a quintessential plot, a quintessential setting, or taking a characteristic to quintessential heights. After all, it wasn't the mean boss who wore Prada, but the devil.

9

Journal to Freedom

"Every time I put my hand to the page, I am altering the energy that flows through my life."
—Julia Cameron

I don't journal. I have excuses for ignoring it. Time. That's the big one. Writing is squeezed in after work and family. So, I want my efforts to produce a complete story, not daily whines, which seem aimless and messy. But as the years go by, ideas fade. Confidence dwindles. Recently, I decided to try mixed-media collage. It's a world of adhesives, color, pattern, and layering. The act of ripping and gluing paper and assembling dissimilar objects to create a new vision is fun. You have the freedom to do anything.

I also noticed a side effect. As I crumple and paste, story ideas bubble up. I'm energized to put words on the page. And then it hit me—when I make mini-collages in my sketchbook, I am journaling. My entries are often aimless and always messy, and they bear the most delicious fruit—inspiration.

As writing teacher Lynn Schwartz discovered, journal writing is a way writers find their voices and gather courage. After all, you can do anything you want to in a journal, like singing in your car or dancing alone in the kitchen, the way my husband did the night our first daughter was born. I was still in the hospital, of course, but he told me about it, and it was easy to imagine him in the 4 A.M. dark, expressing joyous awe and relief in awkward leaps and clumsy spins.

With a journal you can experiment with expressing awe and joy, too, as well as your fear, doubt, regret, and general contrariness. You can think out loud and express yourself freely in figurative leaps and spins.

If you're intimidated by the idea of writing any kind of narrative, start your journal by making a list. List things that you love; people you can't live without; things you would like to understand or to do before you die. List things you wish someone had told you about losing a job or making a commitment, about baking with low-fat sour cream before you had your whole book club over.

List things you'd do if an asteroid was on a collision course with Earth. Enumerate the things your mother told you: *never look at the sun, don't kiss the cat, if you don't stop scowling your face will freeze that way*. List things that you miss and have always missed.

Twenty percent of the population actually suffers from a genetic predisposition for not sadness but longing—a wiring of the brain that generates a pervasive sense of something lost. This subtle sense of something missing can even be for something you never had, like a grandmother who adored you, a faithful dog, or great talent. What do you long for? Can you name it? Can you get it?

Like all writing, journal writing explores and answers questions, solves mysteries, releases anxiety, entertains, absolves guilt, cherishes, and immortalizes, but it is unique in that you know from the outset the intended audience is only you and whoever you invite to listen. You can be writing to yourself, to God, to your dead Aunt Rose, or to your best friend, as long as it is someone with whom you feel safe and accepted without judgment.

So just close your eyes and make some lists. Things you cherish, things you've squandered. Lists bring organization to cluttered thoughts, clarity to murky emotions, and with clarity comes the possibility for growth and change.

When you are ready to go beyond lists and to try a narrative, a journal can be a diary, an essay, a log, a record, a letter to someone you know or someone unseen. It can be a report, a reminiscence, an account of daily events, or a reflection on what happened the day before. You can make your journal a formalized record of a specific time or event—"first year in my baby's life," "last year on the farm."

The irony is that while journal writing is not concerned with the quality of expression, journaling invariably is what all good writing is—a process of discovery in the act of writing itself. Remember: it is the physical act of writing that brings forth ideas. You never need to wait for the idea to come first. If stuck, just look around and describe what is right in front of you. Use description: "It's snowing, the sun is shining, there's a squirrel hanging from the birdfeeder, my desk gleams in the morning light, there goes all the birdseed, I hate those squirrels."

If we never intend to make a journal public, what purpose does it serve? The answer is it serves many purposes writers can make use of. As psychotherapist Virginia Pritchett says:

> In my practice I often advise people to keep a journal. Not only is it cathartic, it also is a place where clients can write out how they solved particular issues they are bound to encounter again. When those problems do rebound, the writer can look back and review what has worked in the past. Some of those journal entries have become profoundly moving poems and vignettes written by people whose original motivation for writing was simply personal growth.

A journal records what might otherwise be lost. We stumble upon insights, feelings we have suppressed, ideas we might not have discovered. Writing down goals cements them in our consciousness, even if we are simply writing about our plans for the day. This is an amazing process and you should try it. Once something is written down, your brain will become your private secretary, drawing your attention to tasks you have pushed aside. It works the same way in which we tend to purchase every item on our grocery list, even though the list is still at home sitting on the empty cat food bag.

Writing about problems gets them out of our heads and literally at arm's distance on the page. Just writing them down implies there's a solution, so a journal generates hope. Writing about joy enhances it the way telling a friend some good news makes the news feel real. Writing about relationships can untangle them. Writing about gratitude feeds your connection to well-being and safety. It's the Coach Santa approach to writing.

Coach Santa taught my daughter Emily to run when she entered high school. Coach took the new runners, the kids who were still coltish and awkward, and turned them loose on the cross-country field. They were all over the place, arms held too high, shoulders tight and hunched, elbows and knees akimbo. Some were running too fast and burning out, others plodding along like Clydesdales. But Coach Santa would fall in place beside a struggling kid and as they ran side by side, begin to tap out the beat of his own heart on his chest. "Hear that?" he'd say. "Run to that." Soon heartbeats would coordinate until all the kids, the tall and the short, the clumpers and the gazelles, were running to the beat of a single heart.

They ran faster and longer and took pride in their endurance. A journal begins by voicing the beat of a single heart. It is a way to find your rhythm, and in time it will connect you to others.

Methods

There are as many methods for writing in a journal as there are forms of meditation. Experiment. Try writing at the same time every day. Most people prefer morning because clearing out the clutter is a nice way to start the day, but you are not bound to that regimen. Many cultures around the world believe that anytime light enters or leaves the world is sacred. Try writing in the late afternoon as the shadows lengthen or at twilight when the whippoorwills call. Write for a set time period—10 to 20 minutes, perhaps. Play music. Create a special place.

Try writing purely stream of consciousness or by focusing on one particular word.

See what you can produce in a three-minute sprint to see if urgency will overwhelm your censor.

Try beginning the day by writing down everything bothering you—even the petty stuff—so that you can be rid of it.

Try interviewing yourself. Ask yourself a question and then answer it. Try writing your responses in your nondominant hand. The question might be huge, like "What do I want?" or specific, like "Why did I feel a flash of anger yesterday when Jane said, 'Call me back'?" Writing in your nondominant hand is not easy. You tend to misspell, cut your responses down to the fewest possible words, and leave words out. Granted, sometimes the writing looks like the cut and pasted letters of a ransom note, but it also has a disarming way of looking as if a child wrote it, which makes it feel incredibly honest. Try memory journaling—writing about things you know by heart (an Emily Dickenson poem, all the state capitals, a jump rope chant, a lock combination) in your nondominant hand. Who taught you these things and why?

Write about early memories, or go through your own history, writing about all your neighbors, or jobs, or recurring dreams. I have a friend whose husband has had nothing but dreams set in high school for the past 30 years. Surely there is material there.

Write letters you will never send. Make them wildly accusatory, forgiving, understanding, confrontational, full of grace.

Try a prompt: Look over your life and list the people in your family you know for a fact have had the least influence on you—like the uncle you rarely saw or the brother who is nine years older. Now imagine the opposite is true. How?

No matter what method you use, write in your journal at a regular time and in a place where you have privacy. Make it a place you enjoy being, a place that feels safe. Start with meditation, music, or an inspirational reading to prime the pump.

Write Like It Will Never Be Read

Every Tuesday night, all summer long, the United States Naval
Academy Band performs free concerts down at the Annapolis City
Dock. Residents bring lawn chairs and set them up in the park that
borders the harbor. They bring their kids, grandparents, babies in
strollers, and the cares of a long day. Tourists perch on pier pilings
or wooden benches as the band sets up, drawn to the electric anticipation in the air. The bricks in the courtyard still hold the heat of
the summer sun, but no one cares. A saltwater breeze from the harbor carries its cooling promise of the coming night.

Because the band is military, its members are in uniform—
midshipmen and -women wearing their dress whites for the occasion.

The lead singer is a beautiful girl, shiny blond hair tucked under
her cap. She welcomes the crowd, her crisp shirt neatly tucked into
the A-line skirt that ends professionally at the top of her knees.
There is a stir of anticipation. Then the drummer starts the beat,
the guitarist joins him, and our conservative young naval officer
breaks into a rousing rendition of Lady Gaga.

But the real show is in front of the stage, where about a dozen
children—most under the age of 6—have gathered. They swing
and sway, they hop up and down in place like tiny lunatics. They are
completely off the beat. They spin like little helicopters that have lost
their stability rudders and fall into each other both unselfconsciously
and without acknowledgment, then clamber to their feet and spin
some more—as if each is dancing to music only he can hear.

It is a purely unchoreographed expression of individuality that is
surprisingly moving. They are so unencumbered by ego or expectation. "To know a thing, dip yourself in it like pen and ink, let it write
you in its own words," says Elizabeth Ayres. Give it a try. Journal to
the music only you can hear.

10
Connection: Making What Happened What Matters

"All things by immortal power near or far, hiddenly to each other linked are, that thou canst not stir a flower without troubling a star."
—Francis Thompson

Sarah Sinclair is a military wife with two young sons who longs to return from the East Coast to the Wyoming grasslands of her youth. Her husband is fulfilling the last year of his military service as an instructor at the U.S. Naval Academy.

Since the family's arrival in Annapolis, Sinclair's world has been partitioned by the high brick walls of the Academy, while the walls containing her childhood were the cedar posts and barbwire fencing of her family's ranch. Once she wanted to escape the rural isolation of her adolescence. Having done so, she wants only to return—to find the opening between the two worlds, a gate.

Sinclair writes of her father's early instruction about the way over obstacles:

My father's gates never dragged in the dirt. They swung unhindered in the wind, slid silently over Wyoming sage brush and snow. But

his was a constant vigil. He never missed our attempts at lazy short-
cuts over the wrong ends of his sturdy gates.

"Climb the fence," he'd say, "Walk around," or occasionally, "Open
the damn thing!" The soil and muck of ranching wasn't pushed
around by the worn-out hinges of an abused gate, but by our
persistent learning curve—eventually we learned that a worn-out
gate was a gate we had to pick up and carry over its normal arc.

Climb a gate at its hinges, the author's father had taught her, at
the place of connection, at the strongest attachment. What you
neglect you will carry. All of these metaphors are embedded in this
very factual description. All of them, when recognized, will allow the
author to deepen her essay and expose insights that touch all of us.

Making the Connection

Besides entertainment, the true gift of any book you read is that it
illuminates your own life through someone else's experience and
imagination. Without hours of therapy, you gain new perspective,
new insight, a new sensibility. But what the reader gains from reading the story is in direct proportion to what the author gains from
writing it. So how do you make those connections yourself as you
write? How do you make a story about what happened, in reality or
in fiction, have any depth?

Find the connection between what happened in the room and
what happened in the heart; reveal an emotional truth even when it
defies the facts. Make what *happened* what *matters*.

One of my students wrote an essay about her irascible 96-year-
old mother. Mother nags, objects, whines, and bullies everyone. She
obsesses over symptoms, belittles the doctors trying to help her, and
has no appreciation for the daughter who dutifully takes her to each
tedious appointment.

While cathartic for the writer, this two-dimensional expression of frustration offers little to the reader until the writer reveals that in the exam room her mother suddenly clutches her chest. With a dismissive sigh borne of her exhaustion and frustration, the daughter says, "Now mother wants the doctor to believe it is a problem with her heart, that she has a *heart* problem." And she does.

Embedded in the facts, the emotional truth of the essay is revealed: the narrator's angry, withholding mother *does* have a heart problem, a problem *of* the heart. Reading this sentence as metaphor is a way intuition decodes the real subject of the essay being telegraphed through the facts.

Foster, don't force, that translation as you work. You will find, however, that connections invariably appear where someone—the author or the character—is vulnerable. Connections lie dormant in your story like seeds planted just below the surface. Look for them where someone fails, fears, stumbles, admits their faults, recognizes someone else's pain, or understands their own accountability or hurt.

These places become apparent when a line written from the left brain is interpreted by the intuitive and evocative right brain. In this case the link between aggravation and loyalty, duty and love, becomes visible as the writer realizes the underlying source of her mother's shortcomings and can forgive them. Connections in writing often are attached to someone's growth.

It is easy to write without recognizing the connection, even when you are the author of it. Once you hear the echo of that deeper level of thought, however, like the essayist writing of her mother, you can illuminate and explore it. With the epiphany that heart damage is what her essay is really about, she can become her own best editor, cutting away what doesn't serve and going deeper and into more detail where it does.

Write with abandon; then re-read, looking and listening for places where you have revealed "spirit in terms of matter," as Frost

said. Read your work aloud, not just to hear places where you have
repeated words, but in order to compensate for your blind spot.
Often you can hear a connection that is invisible to the eye.

Sometimes the connections encoded in a piece of writing shine
through the rubble, but other times, you are so immersed in the
writing you can't recognize the obvious. By putting the work aside
for a time—a few hours, a few days, or a few weeks—you are often
able to see more readily. Sometimes you have to get out of the water
to see the shape of the shoreline. Sometimes someone else has to
point it out.

The process is similar in fiction. The true subject of your story
emerges as your characters encounter obstacles and make choices.
That subject is often a surprise, telegraphed through a simple statement of fact.

This happened to me in the writing of "Turbulence." A mother is
talking to her frustrated daughter on the phone. The teenager has
been visiting colleges out of state. In a few months she will make
the first move toward independence, toward beginning a life of her
own.

The girl's flight home has been cancelled and she is stuck in an
airport a thousand miles away on an indefinite layover. She is angry, rancorous, and both mother and daughter are struggling in the
relationship. The mother wants to hang on even as she needs to let
go; the daughter needs to try her wings, but it is far easier to do so
angry than vulnerable. Her constant criticism of her mother holds
her own ambivalence of the coming change at bay, but she has been
so aggressively difficult to live with that the mother has had to tape
the girl's baby photo to the refrigerator just to remember the love
she can't feel at the moment.

The mother offers to call the airline for the girl, to try to get
some answers about her flights.

I excavate the phonebook from the kitchen junk drawer to look up the number for Continental. Maybe they will tell an adult what's going on or put Sophie on another flight. I honestly hadn't noticed that the layover was three hours or perhaps I read the fine print wrong. Shoving the phonebook a little further away I squint at the tiny numbers. I have been having to hold things at greater and greater distances to see.

It is that last line that reveals the actual subject of a story begun as a description of facts. The mother is going to have to let go, to allow space and distance in order to see the beautiful woman her daughter is about to become. Holding something farther away is sometimes the only way to see it clearly.

That situation is resolved not by pointing to it, but by staying concrete at the end of the story. Trust that the reader will make the connection if you just tell what happened. Resist the urge to explain, to interpret the action.

After several delays due to airport closings and a near crash in stormy weather, the mother in this story finally stands at the airport gate to meet Sophie. By her side is her younger daughter, the easy one, who still finds nothing but delight in her family. As passengers stream down the concourse the mother is lost in thought, searching the faces of strangers for the difficult daughter she loves.

The day before Sophie left for orientation, we made a trip to Bed, Bath and Beyond to buy things she will need in her dorm.

I loaded our packages in the trunk, suddenly aware these were the last days we would ever really live together. On the way home I found myself repeatedly saying, "When I was pregnant with you."

"Would you believe we didn't have air conditioning the summer I was pregnant with you?"

"That was the vacation where I was pregnant with you."

*She was going to say something about it if I didn't stop so
I reviewed impossible facts to distract myself, just as I'd distracted
myself through labor the night she was born.*

*I locate Sophie heading down the concourse in the stream of
disembarking passengers. She is lean and sunburned, as tall as
a woman, her hair tied back like a child's. I stand and wave so
she'll find us.*

We have breathed the same oxygen since the dawn of time.
She sees us. Walks faster.

In a thousand years Cepheus will become the North Star.
She looks confident and so happy. She's waving too.

The earth spins through space in the key of b flat. *She's
laughing, running now.*

Once I was pregnant with you.

It is connection that transforms a flat piece of writing into one
that resonates, wherever that connection is exposed. To make that
connection for the reader, you must discover it yourself. Discover
it in the process of writing, discover it in the facts, in the telling of
what happened, and in the showing of what was felt.

Connection as Catharsis

"One sees great things from the valley, only small things from the
peak," says G. K. Chesterton. Many writers write to process events
in their lives, to give voice to experiences of love and loss, to admit
mistakes, and to experience the relief and the redemption of getting
something out into the healing light of day that has been carried
privately for many years. Perhaps the last role of connection is to
allow *dis*connection: to put experience on the page, bless it, and let
it go.

11

The Secret of Showing
(Don't Tell)

"Don't say it was 'delightful,' make us say 'delightful' when we've read the description. You see, all those words, (horrifying, wonderful, hideous, exquisite) are only like saying to your reader, please will you do my job for me?"
—C. S. Lewis

On the view screen of the Starship *Enterprise*, a mysterious space capsule appears. Jean Luc Picard rises from his captain's chair and moves toward the object to investigate. Suddenly struck by some invisible force, he drops unconscious to the deck of the bridge. Alarmed Starfleet officers hover over him and the doctor is paged.

Over the next hour of this episode of *Star Trek: The Next Generation*, Picard regains consciousness on an unknown planet where he discovers he is a member of an alien civilization. Told that he has been sick, he is slowly nursed back to health by a wife he does not recognize. Although subliminally aware that he is out of his own time and place, he incrementally embraces his new life. He comes to love his wife and the family they create together. He finds a place of meaning within his community by becoming a writer—a chronicler of the events befalling his planet. His children grow up and have children of their own. Now an old man, Picard nears the end of his life while the sun grows hotter, droughts occur more frequently, and the entire civilization edges toward cataclysmic disaster.

At the exact moment of Picard's death, attended by grief-stricken family members on his doomed planet, he regains consciousness on the bridge of the *Enterprise*. The people hovering over him are once again his crew members, who tell him he has been lying unconscious for 20 minutes.

Only Picard knows he has awakened from an experience where he lived out an entire life span of at least 80 years. Ultimately it is discovered that the planet of Picard's dream was obliterated when its sun went nova a million years ago. Forced to choose a way to record their existence, these beings didn't send a global library into space or the works of their finest musicians. They sent forth one perfect, detailed sensory experience in the form of a single lifetime to become part of one human memory. They made their witness a participant in their history, so that he could be a meaningful repository of it.

Like the writers of science fiction who created them, these beings knew that giving the reader an experience is worth a thousand descriptive words.

When you give your reader an experience and let him draw his own conclusions from it, you are showing, not telling, in your writing. This skill is imperative because your reader is far more likely to feel what you want him to feel, see what you want him to see, when you show instead of tell.

History is full of fairy tales, myths, legends, and parables that make their points by showing instead of telling, illustrating instead of lecturing, providing examples instead of dictation. After all, which will you remember most vividly, a birth you witness or a birth announcement? An assault or the report in "Police Beat"? So how do you show instead of tell? What tools can you use?

Present the Evidence

The only way to convince a reader of anything is to let him experience the stimuli and draw his own conclusions. You may not tell your reader how to feel any more than you would tell your best friend how to feel. In dramatizing a moment (another term for writing that shows), you present clues to emotions without labeling them. Where do you find these clues? Take any emotion and ask yourself how it looks and feels within your own body, then put those details on the page.

If you want your reader to know your character is worried, ask yourself what worry looks like. Where is it felt? Think of something that worries you and look in a mirror. What do you see? Perhaps you would write, "John bit his lip, but he could not keep his knee from jiggling." Conclusion? John is anxious and worried, but because you let the reader figure that out without telling him, he is engaged. You have made the reading interactive.

When you want to show an emotion, ask yourself: What do I do when I'm scared? Overjoyed? Surprised? What happens to my heartbeat? Do I suddenly sit down? Jump to my feet? Where in my body do I feel these things? Let your reader see the action, the reaction, but let him infer the emotion and you will have collaborated. Remember that good writing is about revelation.

Suppose you want your reader to understand your character is a complex, angry woman who hides her bitterness beneath a soft and gentle voice that makes it even more lethal. You might write:

She had no friends and her neighbors gave her a wide berth. Children didn't cross her yard without permission more than once and paperboys knew to leave the bill in her mailbox. Her tone of voice was so disarming that it often took several sentences for the listener to realize he was being humiliated or dismissed. Like the time she told the paperboy with tremendous concern in her voice that she'd just hate for him to lose his job because the paper wasn't correctly folded. She had tears in her eyes as she threatened him.

Again: action, reaction, inferred judgment without labeling.

In another example, Camilla Schwarz writes:

I was wide eyed and learning to master the simple stuff when she became my patient for many days in a row. What struck me first were her beautiful hands and long elegant fingers lying purposeless on the blanket. I was new but had been blessed with the ability to leave most of my work at work, but that night, my dark beautiful patient came home with me.

The doctor wanted to perform a procedure that might enable her lung to heal. It involved injecting a caustic substance into the lung via the chest tube and required the assistance of a nurse. It is excruciatingly painful.

Dr. R. dosed her with a few IV shots of valium and Demerol and began his task. At first I held her hand as though we were strangers joined in prayer at the dinner table. As the pain took over, she began to writhe and scream so that my politely offered comfort was but a raindrop on a house fire. My small hands fit easily around her wrists and I pinned her on the bed and sat on her legs.

The author doesn't say, "Nursing is emotionally draining, exhausting, and empathy will just about kill you, burn you out." Instead she presents action and reaction. She puts the reader in the scene with her. Schwarz continues:

When the procedure was over I remained with my patient and had to make her turn from side to side in order to let the medicine coat as much of the lung as possible. She was delirious with pain and with each wave, I became more engulfed until I found myself in bed with her, cradling her, rocking her and crying, my tears so abundant that I wiped them on the top of her hair.

That's what it means to show and not tell. If you are showing your reader something, you cannot be simultaneously preaching, justifying, moralizing. What are other specific hallmarks of showing?

The Clues Are in the Details

Be specific. Write "Lexus" instead of "car," "macadamia-encrusted halibut" instead of "fish," "second-story walk-up" instead of "house." Show by making your details sensory. Remember that your scene is happening in a three-dimensional world—your characters are aware of scents, textures, sounds, and tastes as well as what they see. Avoid adjectives and adverbs and try never to line them up. Adjectives and adverbs are the tools of telling, of description. As Mark Twain said, "If you see an adjective, kill it."

For example, if you want to show "old" by appealing to the senses in describing an abandoned house, do so without using the word:

"The house smelled musty and dank in the lower rooms and the upper rooms smelled dry and stale. Stair treads creaked in protest, as if they hadn't supported more than the weight of a mouse in years. The windows were cracked, opaque puzzles."

"Ah," the reader says, "old house."

Remember that you can enhance your descriptions by the use of simile, and if those comparisons don't come to you organically in the writing, go back and enrich the work by adding them in as part of your editing process.

"Getting to know her again was like reclaiming a house when you've been on a long trip. You freshen the air, fill the rooms with music and light, build a fire, fill the pantry. Gradually, he reestablished his presence in her life."

A good simile or metaphor is one of the fastest ways to signal quality to a reader, but they are also minefields for cliché. Tune

your ear to any phrase that sounds familiar and check it out. If you
have heard it before, it's a cliché. Cut it and find an original way to
convey the same thought. Instead of "cold as ice" ask yourself what
else is cold. "As cold as the mall in July," "as cold as heartache," "as
cold as a tombstone in January," "as cold as the bathroom floor on a
February morning"?

Instead of "his eyes were as blue as the sea," or "as blue as the
sky," which are clichés, think and feel into things that are blue—"his
eyes were as blue as mountains appear at a distance."

Description vs. Action

Let your verbs do the work, and keep them concrete. Be precise
in your choice because as Mark Twain also rightly said, "The right
word to the almost-right word is as lightning is to lightning bug."
Instead of "laugh," try "giggle," "smirk," or "guffaw." Instead of
"run," try "sprint" or "dash." Instead of a passive word like "put," try
"slammed," "slung," or "dropped." Instead of telling the reader your
character is impatient, show it:

"Reshma rushed into the office, flung herself into an empty chair,
and looked pointedly at the grandfather clock."

When you are revising your work and hit a page or two that
seem flat, see if you can show something you have told, flesh out all
summaries, replace a description with action and dialogue. Think of
writing a scene as writing what can be seen, what is happening.

Show your reader emotion by surprising him with your character's reaction. In the movie *The Summer of '42*, a young war bride
waits for her beloved husband in a cottage they've rented on the
Atlantic coast. In her loneliness and isolation, she befriends an
innocent and awkward adolescent boy from town who develops
a crush in response. One evening the boy drops by uninvited
and finds the young wife mute, disheveled, eyes red and swollen,

a crumpled telegram lying on the table, a record turntable silently spinning long after the music has ended.

In the rawness of new grief, in her nearly dissociative state, the young woman leads the boy to bed without a word. As viewers, we have been shown by her actions that her husband has been killed, and by her actions we understand that the young man is a desperate substitution, a heartbroken expression of the new widow's lost love and unbearable pain.

Telegraph an emotion to your reader by the words you embed. In Joyce Carol Oates's famous short story "Where Are You Going? Where Have You Been?" she repeats the word *crazy* over and over as the young female protagonist tries to resist the seduction of a dangerous and strangely charismatic intruder.

Brad Kessler's novel *Birds in Fall* opens with a plane descending into the sea at night. Strewn throughout the description of what is happening in the cabin are words such as uneasiness, dead, strange, oddly, alarm, frozen, unnervingly, shredded, shuddered, burned, even before the reader is fully aware of what is happening.

He heightens the reader's experience with sensory detail as well: the snoring of a passenger blessedly unaware; the *shhh* of the engine; the *pffff* of lifejackets inflating; the drone and rattle of the engines; the smell of vomit, breath mints, and burning plastic. We care because we're *there*.

Showing Character

One of the most important applications of showing writing is to show who a character is rather than tell it. How do we do that?

Dialogue: What does your character choose to talk about? Herself? Other people? Her best friend? Her disappointments? Her joy at working with the homeless? What we talk about is a huge clue to show character. How does your character speak? Quickly? Loudly? Does she use slang? Does she use expressions of the very young? Profanity? Cliché exclamations? Does your character say "Excuse me?" not as a polite request for forgiveness but as a bullying threat? Does she feign an accent? Try to overcome one? Stammer? Interrupt? Are there things she refuses to speak about?

Choices: You show who your character is as well by the choices she makes. Does she take the easy way out? Does she act impulsively—which looks courageous but isn't—or with determination and courage? Does she make sacrifices for others or to get what she wants?

Intentions: You also show by letting your reader know your character's intentions. Does she work at the homeless shelter because she has no skills? Does she work there because it is her nature to help those in need? Or does she work there in order to get a reference to the Alabama School of Social Work?

Memories: Your character reveals clues to who she is by her memories. Was she traumatized, abused, or abandoned and is plagued by these memories? Did she have such a happy childhood that it is difficult for her to empathize with those who didn't? Does she perhaps have trouble remembering parts of her past? What does she *not* remember?

In Tobias Wolff's short story "Bullet in the Brain," a full page details the moments the protagonist will not remember as a bullet makes its deadly pass through his memory. Only then does Wolff show us the single summer afternoon the protagonist *does* remember, and the inclusion of both, what is and is not remembered, shows us the whole man, who he was, what he became, and what he might have been.

Dreams: Character is also shown through dreams—those that are goals and those that literally come to her in the night. Does she laugh in her sleep? Have nightmares? Sleepwalk? Does she want to be Secretary of State? An Evangelical minister? A rich widow? A famous scientist?

Reputation: Is your character trustworthy? An expert in her field? What do other people say about your character? Is she the subject of gossip? Is she admired? Is she reviled? Avoided?

Idiosyncrasies and Habits: Does your character have to be the one to initiate ending every phone call? Does she drive too fast? Does she chew her pencil? Interrupt constantly? Does she always criticize the waiter? Why?

Desire: What does your character want? This revelation not only shows a great deal about who your character is, your plot will rest upon it. If your character wants more than anything to win an Olympic Gold Medal, that demonstrates something about her internal makeup. If she is willing to sacrifice her social life in order to achieve this goal, that is a showing detail as well. If she is willing to sacrifice her integrity, that shows even more.

Hand in hand with your character's desire is your need to show what your character is willing to do to achieve that desire. That is where showing writing allows the character to intersect with the plot. What does she want and what is she willing to do to get it? At what expense?

Where Is It Most Difficult to Show?

Even writers who have managed to stay concrete, to rely on verbs and not adjectives, and to show through specifics often find it difficult to avoid slipping into telling writing at the end of an essay or story. The primary reason is lack of confidence. You must trust your own skill and the reader's sensitivity enough to believe that the reader doesn't need help getting that final message. The impulse to explain, summarize, and wrap up the story is hard to resist, but good writers stay concrete. They continue to render the world around the character to the end of the story. As Scott Russell Sanders shows in this excerpt from *The Paradise of Bombs*, there is no need to explain when you simply reveal.

In this excerpt, the author's family has gathered to see Haley's Comet, and his young son is frustrated, unable to find the comet in the vast expanse of stars on a bitterly cold night. Sanders does not have to say one word about parental love, about the hopes and dreams we carry for our children. He writes instead:

> *I pointed, aimed the binoculars for him, but still he could not find the firefly in the glitter of stars. He was trembling. I squatted down and took his face in my hands to guide his looking and whispered directions in his ear.*

> *"Do you see it now?" My breath cast a cloud about our heads.*

> *"I don't know," he said, his voice raw with frustration. "I can't tell; it's all a jumble. There's too many lights. What if I miss it?"*

> *I felt like weeping, there in the night among strangers, holding my son's face and murmuring in his ear, because I could not see through his eyes, he could not see through mine, and all I had to offer were a few words to draw lines on the darkness. Since it was all I knew how to do, I kept murmuring, stringing words into sentences, sentences into galaxies and constellations.*

> *At length he murmured, "I think I see it. Yes, there it is. I see what you're saying." But whether he saw the comet, or only my words sketched over the darkness, I do not know.*

Onboard the Starship *Enterprise*

There are many places where telling is the best choice in your work. You will tell when you need to move the story forward, or to efficiently convey important factual information. Sometimes it is a matter of variety and pacing: you have been showing for a page or two and the work will benefit from the contrast. It might be that you need to summarize in order to gain momentum in your scene.

Conversely, you may want to write a page or two that tells in order to slow the pace of the action or the intensity of the emotion.

"Good writing is supposed to evoke sensation in the reader—not the fact that it is raining but the feeling of being rained upon," wrote E. L. Doctorow. Showing and telling both have a place in your work, but every time you show your reader something you want him to see, you imprint an experience into his memory that will remain vivid long after words, and even worlds, are forgotten.

12

On Location:
Setting and Place

*"At its best, setting itself becomes a character interacting with
other characters."*
—Noah Lukeman

*Grant Avenue was a narrow, unlined road. We drove slowly along it
until we arrived at two gray stone pillars supporting an open, black
wrought-iron gate. EDEN was engraved on one pillar and HALL
on the other. My perspiration-stained dress, chosen because it would
travel well, peeled off the seat as I leaned forward to get a better view.*

*A lush green hockey field shaded by a line of leafy oaks took my
mind off my dress. I rolled the window down and inhaled the scent of
newly cut grass baking in the sun. Then, little by little, the rose-colored
mansion began to emerge from the pines. We passed a statue of Saint
Michael, reached the circular drive, and the school loomed in front of
me. Long brown arms of fieldstone topped with multiple spires and
crosses—rows of vacant windows that stared silently back at me. The
tall dark figure of a nun standing at the top of the stairs waved us
around to the rear of the building with a white handkerchief. I entered
Eden Hall for the first time through the back door.*

—Betty Driscoll

The scent of newly cut grass, a damp dress, vacant windows like staring eyes: settings can be easily visualized because when written well, they appeal to all our senses. We will remember a setting long after the details about exactly what happened and to whom have faded. This is particularly true when strong emotions are evoked in a particular setting. In times of stress, the brain releases a chemical that acts like a fixing agent, mentally photographing your environment. This is why nearly everyone can tell you where they were when the World Trade Center fell or they heard of the *Challenger* disaster.

Setting is to story what memory is to experience—a distilled essence that exceeds the limitations of space and time.

A Versatile Multitasker

Often overlooked, setting can be the dominant element in a story, as it is in the children's classic *The Secret Garden* by Francis Hodgson Burnett. I read this book decades ago and remember a sickly boy confined to a wheelchair and a young girl forced by circumstance to join his household at Misselthwaite Manor. Amazingly, I'd forgotten major elements of the narrative itself: the boy feared he was becoming a hunchback and Mary, the protagonist, had lost her parents in a cholera epidemic. What had remained in memory was the *garden* with its high, concealing, ivy-covered walls, its secret rusty key, and its tangles of overgrown vines. Setting had dominated the book's impact, even subjugating plot and character.

When Mary first discovers it, the garden has been untended for a decade. The roses, left to proliferate, have grown out of control, yet they make the garden appear magical even in its state of neglect.

> *There were other trees in the garden, and one of the things which made the place look strangest and loveliest was that climbing roses had run all over them and swung down long tendrils which made*

light swaying curtains, and here and there they had caught at each other or at far-reaching branches and had crept from one tree to another and made lovely bridges of themselves.

Over the course of the book, the orphaned Mary transforms the garden into a sanctuary of lush new growth. The setting now brims with color.

The place was a wilderness of autumn gold and purple and violet blue and flaming scarlet and on every side were sheaves of late lilies standing together—lilies which were white or white and ruby. . . . Late roses climbed and hung and clustered and the sunshine deepening the hue of the yellowing trees made one feel that one stood in an embowered temple of gold.

The wheelchair-ridden boy and virtually every other character in the book, including Mary, are being transformed as well. Neglect and loss are transcended and replaced with health and rediscovery. The setting is reflecting the action and serving as a metaphor for the plot. A secret garden is the perfect container for a story about rebirth.

Mirroring and Amplifying Emotions

Setting can predispose the reader to feel what the character feels. It can also change the entire nature of an interaction by virtue of changing the visual context.

Imagine a boy and his father deep in conversation. The father is sharing a profound belief in God. It is a conversation that reveals important aspects of the father's personality and the nature of his relationship with his son. It is a showing device that demonstrates the intimacy and intensity of the bond between them. Place the conversation on a creaky front porch swing where the two are watching the sun set over the cornfields and it has a fairly benign effect. Move the conversation to an airport terminal just before the son's deployment to the Middle East and it takes on another layer of significance. Now make that conversation a monologue whispered to an unconscious son in a hospital intensive care unit and it takes on new nuance and meaning.

How a setting is described can be an intensely personal perspective yet broad in focus, sketching in an entire landscape or country. As Annie Dillard writes in *An American Childhood*:

> When everything else has gone from my brain—the President's name, the state capitals, the neighborhoods where I lived, and then my own name and what it was on earth I sought, and then at length the faces of my friends, and finally the faces of my family—when all of this has dissolved, what will be left, I believe, is topography: the dreaming memory of land as it lay this way and that.

But setting can also be as narrow in focus as a room, as intimate as the interior of a car or a shared sofa.

Setting as Character and Plot

More than a container for the story, setting can become a character. Take *Room: a Novel* by Emma Donoghue. From the story's outset, the two main characters—a mother and her 5-year-old son, Jack— are held captive within an 11-foot square prison, a room built by the mother's kidnapper. It is Jack's entire world. He was born in Room. He speaks of Room without the preceding article "the," and the word is always capitalized. Thus Room becomes a proper noun; their prison a character whose name is Room. The boy doesn't even know a reality beyond their cell exists. His mother, through her love and imagination, creates a self-contained universe within the walls that simulates normalcy. Room also becomes the plot, however, when Jack's mother realizes they must escape from Room now, or surely die.

A book like *Swiss Family Robinson*, or a film like *Cast Away*, also demonstrates how location not only amplifies emotion and gives context to the action but becomes plot. In each case the setting is the antagonist, and the protagonist must interact with it constantly in order to survive. The setting is the obstacle to be overcome, the conflict to be resolved, the tension that never goes away. In *Cast Away*, a deserted island in an isolating ocean is so powerful an opponent that the protagonist tries to commit suicide in order to escape it. In A. C. Oliver's *A Southern Introduction*, the setting has the opposite effect. The ocean is a drug, a lure, repeatedly enticing the narrator into the seductive crush of its embrace.

> *I follow the large set waves as they grab onto the point and wrap back tightly around the cliff face and I see how the second, and biggest wave of the set, carries more true south in it than the rest and watch it teasingly crest before shacking up in the shallow middle section, throwing itself forward, then doubling over, top to bottom, with the foam now flying off the back like a giant bridal train.*

> *My timing is off and I know this one is going to hurt as I hurl myself under in bad form and it's going to be bad, real bad, and I feel the pressure build and the roar and fluctuations in the calm, but I escape its rolling back unscathed. ... Neptune's song is low, deep and soft, and the sun is a high, white light, and all of it aches and pulls like a child on your coattails, like a bad addiction, and it is a bad addiction.*

Setting, like character, can also be a linking mechanism. It can be used to tie a whole series of essays or stories together. *Olive Kitteridge* by Elizabeth Strout, for example, is unified not just by character but by the fact that each story's setting is the same small coastal town in Maine. Laura Ingalls Wilder's classics, *Little House on the Prairie* and *Little House in the Big Woods*, are also defined by place.

Creating Memorable Settings

If you are going to set your story at the North Pole, don't include penguins. They live at the South Pole. If your wayfaring sailor is adrift off the coast of Australia, he's not searching for the North Star to orient himself; he's scanning the heavens for the Southern Cross. Research for accuracy.

Books can start with detailed settings before a character even comes on stage: a downpour, an abandoned mill town, an empty nursery. But it is not necessary to download setting all at once. Let your setting materialize gradually and come into focus one element at a time. Let it evolve organically as your story unfolds.

Try using a character to reveal your setting as he surveys the landscape. He notices the rope swing on the hickory tree, the blue front door that a dog has gouged scratching to get in, the dirt yard with the half barrels of red geraniums.

Or allow something inanimate to animate your setting. Follow light as the sun rises to reveal the objects in a room, the sleeping compartment on a train. Let darkness narrate your setting as it settles over a prison or plantation. Let the wind drift in through an open window to caress a photograph, freshen air left stale from a recent fire.

Perhaps a cat wanders through the room revealing detail. It jumps on the mantel, padding along it beneath the oil painting of a ship under sail in its wide gilt frame. It leaps to a mahogany desk where a pair of tortoiseshell glasses are knocked from the green felt blotter to the floor. It startles as the grandfather clock strikes midnight, jumps to the Oriental rug where it stretches, leaps up into a wingback chair with worn upholstery. But be selective with your details. Discrimination is an art. As editor Nadja Maril says:

> As a child, I would follow my father, the artist Herman Maril, to
> his studio to watch him work. I always recognized the scene and

subject, but knew his paintings were nothing like photographs. He was intentionally selecting what he chose to depict on the canvas. Simplicity made a stronger statement. I sift through my observations as a writer, putting into words only what is essential to tell the story.

Character-Specific Detail

A child will describe a setting as he sees it—from a height perhaps 3 feet off the floor. Someone depressed will reveal a setting as he sees it—in grays and browns. Someone who has just received good news will see a setting expansively with vibrant colors, or will focus on the phone for sharing his news, or, perhaps, fling open the door. Someone anxious will see less, someone bored will see more. And sometimes we see through the lens of memory, as writer Ann Jensen does here:

> *In the dim light from the shaded windows, I saw the room I remembered from childhood. My mind let me see what I wanted to see; the graceful lines and deep patina of mahogany furniture, the multi-tiered chandelier with its light-splintering prisms, brightly flowered china bowls, age-burnished brass lamps on shelves and tabletops. I found the button for the light. The feeble glow of the chandelier, denuded of most of its crystal, was cast back into the room by the tall, gilt pier mirror across the room. It leaned precariously over its marble-topped base, testing hidden restraints that held it to the wall. The sickly light was just enough to destroy the shadows and, with them, the room that memory had created for me.*

Make your supporting details as specific as possible: crown molding along the ceiling, a smudged light switch, creaking floor boards, a plant that needs watering, grit on a windowsill.

What scents permeate your setting? Is the air thick with the aroma of garlic from the Chinese restaurant below the apartment?

Is the scent of land drifting to sailors still 20 miles at sea? What can be heard? Church bells? Clinking glasses? Birdsong? Fog horns? What can be touched? Is the desk smooth? Are the stucco walls rough, the quilt worn and soft? What can be tasted?

What is the climate like? Is there a drought? A windstorm? A tidal wave? How about the climate in the room? Is it steamy? Freezing? Suffocating? Maybe it is out of the ordinary—like a cold snap in Florida or downtown Honolulu. Have your narrator react to the setting—close the window, put on a sweater, open an umbrella.

Let the setting initiate action. If your story has taken place inside, take it outside. Change the season. If you are stuck in a scene, try moving your characters to a new setting just to see what they'll do. Move your husband and wife to a Sunday School parking lot, put your arguing sisters on a train, move the family reunion to a ski cabin where there is no snow.

When I was in elementary school, one of my favorite books was *The Wonderful Flight to the Mushroom Planet* by Eleanor Cameron. I remember very little about the plot or the characters—something about a kid my age building a spaceship and the discovery of distressed aliens with huge heads. But I remember the tiny planet the way you can recall a former school but not your classmates, a street you lived on but not the neighbors.

The mysterious planet is a miniature moon called Basidium, held in an invisible orbit above Earth. Moss softer than flower petals covers the ground and mushrooms sprout overhead as imposing as trees. It is a secret world, like the secret garden, a setting created with imagination and skill. It seemed so real, the mushroom planet. When the stars are bright I look for it still.

13

Character and the Cargo Hold: Using the Past

"Most important to understand about the old brain is that it exists outside of time: it makes no distinctions as to why or where or when something happened."
—Harville Hendrix, Ph.D.

One night on a beach in her sixteenth summer, Meredith Hall's life was changed forever by "a boy from away who said love." Years later the incident and its aftermath became the subject of "Shunned," Hall's account of the complete erasure of her world when her resulting pregnancy became public knowledge. Ostracized by every single person in her 1966 small-town community, the trajectory of her life was permanently altered. "Even now I talk too much and too loud, claiming ground, afraid that I will disappear from this life, too, from this time of being mother and teacher and friend," she writes.

Using the Moments That Shape Us

The sibling who protected you from bullies, the friend who saved you from isolation, the teacher who saw into your soul, all contributed to who you became. But so did the coach who humiliated you, the girlfriend who deceived you, the roommate who betrayed you. We just don't like to think about these influences. We tend to file them away quickly and move on. But their impact remains, and with it their potential to serve our writing. When you learn how to use the memories you would rather avoid, you may find they hold within them some of your most important material. The story only you can tell is most likely the story you need to write.

Is there a moment, perhaps shoved to the bottom of memory, when you became you? Is there a moment in time when everything changed? A moment after which nothing was ever the same? Are there three such moments? Have you been trying to leave them behind?

I was on a flight recently from Dulles to LAX. It was the day after a major ice storm in the East had closed a third of the nation's airports and the airlines were playing catch-up. Our flight was delayed, all of us already onboard, waiting to leave the gate. Our pilot came on the intercom, giving periodic updates as to our status.

"Folks, we're ready to push off here, but we've been told we have to wait for thirteen pieces of luggage. We'll be taking off as soon as we've got those bags on board." But over the next fifteen minutes the captain became more irritated with every update. Finally he reported, "Uh folks, we're not waiting anymore."

The cabin lights dimmed and the plane rocked slightly then began the slow push back, the careful turn, the taxi toward the runway. We rolled toward take-off, guide lights whipping by, each passenger in his own way preparing for that moment when the front wheels leave the earth. It is a moment of relief and subtle exhilaration not unlike the one when you know a story-start is going to take flight.

But instead of lift-off, the plane suddenly decelerated and powered down to a stop. After a moment the pilot came on the radio again and explained: "Folks, Air Traffic Control isn't happy about us leaving without the bags. Looks like we're going to sit in a penalty box for a while."

That's the thing about baggage—about the knowledge and experiences you've stuffed, the feelings you've checked and stowed. That baggage is perhaps your most authentic material, and leaving it behind may cost you the stories you were born to write.

The Whole Story Is the Only Story

In an essay titled "Under the Influence," Scott Russell Sanders confronts a subject that haunted him for decades.

> *My father drank. He drank as a gut-punched boxer gasps for breath, as a starving dog gobbles food—compulsively, secretly, in pain and trembling. I use the past tense not because he ever quit drinking but because he quit living. That is how the story ends for my father, age sixty-four, heart bursting, body cooling and forsaken on the linoleum of my brother's trailer. The story continues for my brother, my sister, my mother, and me, and will continue so long as memory holds.*

A lot of fathers drink. And Sanders, like so many children who grew up in traumatic circumstances, will never know who he might have been had his adolescence not been hijacked by his father's illness. Like Hall, Sanders wrote a critically acclaimed essay when finally, decades after the fact, he shared his experience on the page.

Patricia Hampl also stowed the past for many years. As a child, Hampl was ashamed of her Czech grandmother, who could not read or write in English. Hampl wrote her grandmother's correspondence for her, eventually teaching her to at least sign the letters with her own name: "Teresa." The day came when the young Hampl taught her pupil to write "Love" as well, but neglected to explain that a comma should separate the words. At the bottom of the letter a scrawled signature commanded "Love Teresa." Years later Hampl surrendered, and the grandmother she'd resisted writing about became the heroine of a novel. "She wrote it first," Hampl says: "'Love Teresa.'" And in an essay the author titled, "The Need to Say It," she finally did.

Under the Influence

"As a writer, your mind is your palette, and unfortunately your mind stores a lot of baggage," says literary agent Noah Lukeman. Sometimes the stuffed experience is less dramatic but no less formative: a sibling rivalry, a workaholic parent, sudden loss of status, unemployment, poverty. Sometimes there is no specific memory, only a vague feeling. The process of confronting what haunts you enriches the work, but digging a little deeper allows the work to enrich you. Learn to possess your subject, rather than to be possessed *by* your subject. How?

"The subconscious mind works like a computer program that was installed without your knowledge," says author and psychologist Natalie Reid. But your consciousness is riddled with clues. If the smell of Ivory soap inexplicably makes you anxious, open up your memory and explore it on the page. If a co-worker who complains about her dog fills you with out-of-proportion rage, take it to the page. If spring makes you melancholy, stop and review the springs of your past. As a writer, figuring out *why* you feel *what* you feel is like having a thousand writing prompts. Stories and novels evolve from such epiphanies. As Chekhov said, "If you want to work on your art, work on your life."

Nothing is arbitrary. If you loathe the color purple, there's a reason. If the smell of broccoli makes you nauseous, there's a reason. Respect the mysteries and explore them. Let your characters resolve them.

The pilot comes back on the intercom where we sit in the penalty box. "Okay, they've brought the bags out, but now we are waiting for the new weight calculations." He is clearly unhappy. Maybe someone is waiting for him in L.A.; a friend, a wife, a lover. But the weight of your bags is critical to your writing. It's about balance.

Writing about the past heals and transcends it, but with the *whole* story, you can transform it.

Ways to Use the Past

Take what happened and rewrite it as you would like to see it have turned out. Make people more accountable, more courageous, more self-aware than they actually were. Make something happen when nothing did. Expose secrets in a way that benefits a whole town. The exercise is constructive, freeing, and sets a whole new energy in motion. The farther the imagined scenario is from reality, the more liberating it is—the fate you actually experienced appears more arbitrary, impermanent, and less personal.

Combine two of your siblings into one composite character. Take your brother's habit of thinking out loud and give it to your protagonist. Then show his sister coming to value the habit when it illuminates a problem she wants to resolve. Take in the fact that what you invent on the page you may be able to re-create in your life. Examine your mother's loneliness, your father's courage, your neighbor's treachery, and ask yourself "What if?"

Asking "What if?" allows you to stop censoring, to push beyond the subliminal limits of what happened to entertain a more compassionate story. As Lukeman says, "It is your job to clear the slate, to create a sacred space in your mind just for the writing, free from all your neuroses as a person."

Invent reasons people behaved the way they did. Maybe you'll stumble on an actual truth or at least a new empathy. Have your characters make brilliant choices, or forgive bad ones. Your story can hold the tension of ambiguity and the best and worst of all you have known. In this world, however, you can bestow miracles.

Write an ending that is smarter than you are and release it into the world to entertain and inspire others. At the same time, you have just mapped satisfaction, maybe even joy.

Neuroscientists now believe that the primal brain, that ancient, reptilian, "old brain" that Harville Hendrix speaks of, cannot distinguish between "self" and "other." It sees all action as inner-directed. So when we criticize others, bizarrely, *we* feel criticized. When we gossip about a co-worker, *we* feel diminished. And as writers, when we lead a character to an epiphany, laughter, insight, forgiveness, compassion, we feel oddly as if those gifts have been bestowed upon us. What a life-altering combination of fiction and reality! Each informs and transforms the other.

So again, tell the whole story. Show where the laughter comes from, but also show the hands that shook, the tears that were denied, the *bafflement* of those who did harm. Commit to honesty, to showing the whole picture, without judgment, in all its multifaceted glory. In the words of Claude Levi-Strauss, "I am the place in which something happened."

It's okay if you take off late, if waiting until you are ready to write about a particular subject, person, or experience delays the writing of your essay, story, or novel. Meredith Hall published "Shunned" 39 years after her sixteenth summer. Sanders had a 10-year-old son of his own before he wrote about being the 10-year-old son of his tormented father. And Hampl didn't write about her grandmother until she'd written about everything else she could think of.

It is one of those paradoxes of nature: On the wings of truth, lost time is recovered in the air.

14

Plot: What's the Problem?

"Something happened."
—Adage defining plot

I am not asleep. I may look like I am, but that is only so she will not talk to me. I am on our bed. I do have my eyes closed, but I am as alert as ever. I am raw nerve ending, I am one giant eardrum. She walks quickly and decidedly towards the stairs turning off lights as she goes and I imagine she is scared of the dark behind her. I can actually hear her not looking back. She pretends to try to be quiet but she wants me to wake up so I can see her tidying up my strewn-about clothes. When I awake in the morning and get dressed in the dark, I will not know where they are. I will think back to this moment and blame one of us, probably her.

—A. C. Oliver, *First Thing in the Morning*

A plot is a problem. Its solution is a story. Plots develop as characters develop, but they begin in tension, no matter how overt or how subtle.

For many writers, "plot" brings up unpleasant associations, like the words "calculus" and "outline." We would rather not have to think about the plot and just get on with the good stuff—characters and descriptions. What makes plot overwhelming is thinking that you have to have it all figured out from the outset. Be kind to yourself. Just like subject, you don't have to know where you are going in order to begin. But whether you are writing fiction or nonfiction, you must have a succinct sense of the problem to be explored and the ability to articulate it both to yourself and others.

Plot and the Pitch

"Nothing that ends in *palooza* can be good," my husband said. My college had sent a notice to alumni that on the third Saturday in October, the English Department was hosting a "Pitchapalooza," a discussion panel consisting of a New York editor, a literary agent, a best-selling author, and a small press publisher. Any student or graduate with a writing project was welcomed to "pitch" the project to the panel for critique.

The notice was a bit vague about the pitch part, so I called. I was told that there would be a microphone set up in the center of Hodson Hall from which each person with a book idea would address the panelists and other attendees simultaneously. Then the experts would offer advice. What I didn't know until I got there was that you had exactly 60 seconds to make your case, to pique the panel's interest, to explain your book's purpose and proposed reading audience. Sixty *seconds*. It was brilliant in reality, because what the time limit really meant was that you only had the floor long enough to describe your book's plot. The plot was all that mattered, and it quickly became obvious that when the panel said 60 seconds, they didn't mean 61. There was a guy with a stopwatch, which he wielded without love.

Prospective authors tried talking very fast, but no one could understand them and they'd have to sit down, having squandered their opportunity. Other writers' descriptions trailed off when they realized that their books actually had no plots. Some of the more extroverted attendees tried projecting charm in place of substance. It was cringeworthy. Finally the younger undergraduates in attendance started getting up and sputtering spin lines inspired by their desperation and the last movie they'd seen. "Hello! My book is … *Eat, Pray, Love* meets *Pirates of the Caribbean!* No, dude! Chill! (A desperate command to the guy timing.) My book is more … *Finding Nemo* meets … *Titanic!* Wait! It's …"

"Time's *up!*" the moderator would chortle, brandishing his stopwatch. The kind and perplexed panel would look with dubious hope at the next candidate as the previous one stumbled back to his seat, where people who hadn't had their turn yet would whisper, "That was really good."

As ghastly as this experience was, it proved to be a useful tool. It showed the importance of plot and just how necessary it is that you have a distilled version as your touchstone as you write. If you can't narrow your book, essay, or story down to a one-line plot, you probably haven't fully clarified it in your own mind. As an example, pick up any list of best-sellers, such as the one published in *The New York Times*, or take a look at the one-line descriptions of television shows in your newspaper's daily listings: "Lord Helmsly loses his heir." "A woman goes to war against bedbugs." See if you can write out your plot in no more than three sentences and tape them up near your computer. It's like wearing a safety harness on a sailboat in rough seas. You are free to put your attention on other duties, like attending to dialogue or setting, without falling overboard. Plot tethers you to purpose.

Plots take surprising twists and turns as characters take on lives of their own and surprise you with their choices. If you have figured out every aspect of your plot before you begin, you discourage your own spontaneity and creativity and you run the risk that the audience has figured it out as well.

If we are really intimidated by the subject, we look for ways to cozy up to plot. We tell ourselves that plot evolves naturally (it can) and that tension in a story will suffice. Eventually we buy books from the writing reference section that analyzes plots of classic movies and novels. We continue to search for definitions that will simplify the subject, like "*Plot is what happens next.*" "*Plot is obstacles set in your protagonist's way.*" "*There are only two plots: someone goes on a trip and a stranger comes to town.*" One of my favorites is Jim Thompson's explanation: "*There is only one plot. Things are not as they seem.*"

We are also told to think of plot as conflict, crisis, resolution. Sometimes plot is reduced to action, background, crisis, solution. Or it is organized as action, re-action, (repeat as necessary). But the simplest way to *see* the way a plot works is to pick up any children's story.

The Easy-Reader Plot

Children won't wait through long descriptions in which nothing happens. They demand to know the main character's problem on page one. Then they want to know how he's going to get out of his predicament but, perversely, they *want him to fail.* (This is, in fact, their favorite part.) They are particularly delighted if each failure sets the main character dramatically *further back* from his goal. Preschool readers want things to look hopeless right up to the moment of catastrophe. Then they want the hero to dig deep, make a heroic choice, and triumph over adversity. They'll want these exact same things as the adults they become, which is why learning plot from a children's book works so well.

In *A Duck So Small*, written by A. H. Benjamin and illustrated by Elisabeth Holstien, Duffle Duck has a problem: he's unusually small. Being different makes him feel inferior and miserable.

What does Duffle Duck want and what will he do to get it? He wants acceptance. To get it he tries to copy the skills of other birds. Of course (yippee) he fails. For every step he takes toward earning respect, he takes two steps back. Again, this is the sleight of hand of a master plot: to move your protagonist closer to his goal while apparently moving him farther away.

Duffle Duck is too small to dive like the kingfisher.

He is too small to stand on one leg like a heron.

He is too small to peck a hole like a woodpecker.

Then, just when things look the bleakest: crisis! And like all crises, this is the moment that will demonstrate Duffle's substance. Remember, character is revealed through action, but most clearly through the action your character takes under pressure. A baby duck is stuck in a hole in the river bank and all the other birds' beaks are too big to affect a rescue. A life is in jeopardy. The stakes are huge.

Now being small, previously perceived as a weakness, has become a strength. Only the heroic Duffle Duck is small enough to save the baby.

As you get comfortable with the basic formula for plotting, you can add layers and subplots. You can weave several storylines together and let them intersect. If you get stuck or it feels as if you are arbitrarily moving your characters around without forward momentum, remember this: Plot is not random. It's causal.

Because Mary misses the bus, she misses her job interview. Because Mary misses the job interview, Mary doesn't get the job. Because Mary doesn't get the job, Mary is available to crew on a yacht race across the Atlantic. Because Mary is on the boat, she is not able to come to her dying mother's bedside. Everything is cause and effect—on the action level and on the emotional level. We need relationship. We need causality. As E. M. Forster is often quoted: "A story is: 'The King died, the Queen died.' A plot is 'The King died, the Queen died of grief.'"

Plot in Nonfiction

By the time it was my turn at the microphone at Pitchapalooza, the room was sweltering. It was a lot like being in the audience of a grade school talent show when everyone else's kid has already performed and the show's running long. Restless shuffling, gazing around, whispering.

I had written a memoir about the worst year in my life and how I had transformed it into the most spectacular year imaginable. I probably should have just said that and sat down. Instead, I began with my healthy son's out-of-the-blue diagnosis of an incurable illness, living 12,000 miles away with no health insurance, sudden abandonment, a silent and empty house, a forfeited job. I was just warming up.

I was setting the stage with my list of catastrophes. Plot was my punch line. Just as I was getting to my explanation of the creative experiment that changed everything, I heard "Time's up!" I glanced up and saw that the entire panel had been transfixed—only now that the spell was broken they looked like witnesses to a mugging who don't know if help arrived in time. The agent actually looked alarmed, which was not the look I was going for.

Plus, I was embarrassed that I had had to be cut off instead of stopping on my own, although I had no minute hand on my watch. As someone who actually turns my cell phone off at gas pumps, to have broken a rule and been publically disciplined for it was mortifying. But it was a good way to learn that memoirs and essays need plots as well as fiction. If not a conventional plot, nonfiction at least needs an arc of tension, mystery, a question addressed if not resolved. And it needs to be alluded to in short order.

Just as in fiction, essays need action, musings need a point, reminiscence needs a parallel that matters in the present, matters enough to be worth telling. Crisis is an excellent component as well. And in essay, just as in fiction, plot operates on two levels. There is what is happening in the physical world and what is happening in the emotional world of the narrator in response.

Cynthia Gorney is a former *Washington Post* contributor who now teaches. Gorney let her nonfiction plot reveal itself on both levels as she wrote about one moment, a singularity, "in the early part of summer, when the apricots come to the orchards up by the Sacramento River delta." The essay was titled "One Jam Thing After Another—One Woman's Parable of Modern Life and 92.5 Pounds of Apricots."

> *I started making jam because my friend Carol came over one day with some chutney she had made. It was incandescent chutney, and in fact had already won first prize at that year's county fair, but what really bowled me over was the fact that it came in little jars, and Carol had put it there.*

Gorney is setting up a plot in the most conventional way: showing *what someone wants and what she is willing to do to get it.*

> *When the sun hit the kitchen, a kind of rich rose light filled the jars and you could see the curve of things inside, small pepper strips and chunks of peach. I began to covet these jars. ... I wanted to see entire shelves filled end to end with fruit the color of stained glass, and I wanted also to know I had put it there.*

And so it was that one day in early summer Gorney found herself with close to 100 pounds of apricots from which to make jam. She notes that her husband, who might have saved her from this overindulgence, had missed this particular fruit-picking run with the kids. The long day became night as the jam making continued. Gorney chopped and stirred for hours, singing along to Huey Lewis tapes, stacking jars like exquisite jewels up on the shelves before they'd even dried. She was, she freely admits, insufferable with delight.

> *There was so much jam that the shelf could hardly hold it all. I made a double row and stacked the jars, one on top of the other. Then I stood back and looked at the top shelf jam, and did a little dance.*

Then I turned my back.
And then the shelves fell.
All of them. All the shelves.

… It was an amazing noise. It went on for a very long time.

Plots turn at moments of crisis—moments of a character's greatest vulnerability—and are often followed by an epiphany of some kind. In this case, writer and reader come to understand that this experience has been about something other than jam.

My husband, who had covered the entire distance from the living room sofa to the kitchen in one leap, looked at the kitchen floor and then looked at me. My five-year-old son was looking at me too, since he had never before seen a grownup crying and kicking the walls and my husband instantly steered both of us into the dining room. "I'll take care of it," he said.

After a time I came back in to help, but … I started to cry again. My husband had assumed the manner of a paramedic and suggested politely I go somewhere else; late that night, after he had carted out the shards and mopped the floor with lemon-scented ammonia, he told me some of the jars were still intact.

"If you hadn't been here," I said, "I would have taken the children and checked into a hotel."

"I know," he said.

I looked out the window for a while, thinking about the fragility of some arrangements and the ferocious strength of others, and we slept.

Plot can be intricate, violent, intense, but a plot can also be this: a woman wants to create something delicate with her own two hands; something of substance, like incandescent jars of jam, like a marriage. In her enthusiasm, she overburdens the support meant to hold it all. The shelves give way; the marriage holds fast. The plot becomes a revelation about what sustains us.

Sometimes you can change a good story to a brilliant one simply by changing the way in which you structured the plot. Whereas in the preceding essay there is a chronological progression to the narrative arc, you don't have to be tied to that convention. Try shifting the order in which you reveal your plot. Doris Kamenetz, in "Before and After," *begins* with the narrator's moment of greatest vulnerability, the height of the arc of tension.

> *The rap on the door of my motel room comes just as I am pondering what I should do to pass the last few hours of this day. At the door is Mr. L., the man from the room next door. I let him in but I hesitate about what to do once he is standing by the foot of the bed. Mr. L is a man accustomed to his own authority, however, and gets directly to the point.*
>
> *"Would you kiss me?" he asks, his eyes flat black discs.*
>
> *The room is flashing yellow then red, as the stoplight issues orders outside the streaked window. I see the two of us suddenly as if I too am beaming in from the outside: a slight girl of nineteen with wispy hair, her head tilted obliquely on the axis of her long neck, a stocky, fifty-something-year-old man. Behind them, an enormous bed, looming. Had he been led to believe dinner would progress to an evening of intimacy?*
>
> *"No," I say aloud to him but the boundaries of a third question begin to form. What if he doesn't leave? But he does. Curtly, he says goodnight, walks out and I never see him again. That's how the story ends. Here's how it begins.*

Now, having gotten our attention, Kamenetz begins to weave the tale that precedes this moment. It is the story of a young girl whose boyfriend is in a terrible hiking accident, stranding him in a small-town hospital where the girl must wait overnight for a way back home. The boy's father, a diplomat, flies in to assess the damage and then decides to take advantage of the narrator's vulnerability. The real end of the story, so creatively plotted, is when the boyfriend's bandages finally come off and the former sweetness of his good looks has been forever altered. The romance is over by then, and the boyfriend thinks it's humorous that his former endearing smile has healed into a subtly menacing sneer. He dismisses the sad fact that his innocence has been scarred by circumstances beyond his control, but of course he only knows about the loss he can see in the mirror. Kamenetz concludes:

> *He doesn't know what else he has lost, because I don't ever tell him. I think that would be too much even for him to bear.*

Transformation/Illumination

Whether you are writing fiction or nonfiction, one thing your plot should ultimately accomplish is change of some kind. Someone or something needs to be different because of the events that take place in your story. Transformation itself is a form of resolution. A duck gains self-respect. Generosity illuminates deeper appreciation of a marriage. A young girl loses her innocence and chooses silence as an act of compassion.

My college is in a small rural town about 60 miles from where I now live. On the way home from the Pitchapalooza, I spent a lot of time looking out the window as my husband drove. I gazed at fields of harvested corn—a landscape where the bounty of the growing season had been safely gathered in. We covered the miles attended only by our thoughts and an autumn moon. I reflected upon the beauty of the world and all I had to be grateful for: that I would never see any of those people again and that no one would remember my name. Also, I realized, I had learned a lot. You can create multidimensional characters, a compelling setting, authentic dialogue, and beautiful metaphors. But of all the elements of craft necessary to tell a story, it is the plot, the *problem*, that propels a story.

15
What's So Funny?

"Among those whom I like, I can find no common denominator, but among those whom I love, I can; all of them make me laugh."
—W. H. Auden

Laughter heals; it can change the flavor of tears. When our cat died after nineteen years with us, my family was stricken with grief. The cat was put to sleep at the vet's office. My brothers and I prepared to bury the cat. The former cat was in a plastic bag inside a cooler. We dug a hole near the woods where the cat loved to hunt rabbits. Everyone was crying. When we diggers rested for a moment, my father prepared to deposit the cat in the hole. But we weren't done, the hole was too shallow, and my brother shouted, Wait! Don't let the cat out of the bag!

Many things are laughable only later, after everything has turned out fine and we can reflect on our good fortune or our dumb luck. Such as my son's many trips to the emergency room for foreign objects in his nose: raisins, rubber, paper, a toy snake's tail. "See," I once overheard a nurse telling her coworker when she saw my son, "I told you it would be him."

Patrick Madden, who teaches at Brigham Young University, writes of the laughter that shows up in the most unlikely places, like emergency rooms and funerals. When it does, it provides a powerful form of alchemy. Writing that makes us laugh is as effective as music at altering a mood and connecting strangers, but it is rarely a part of writing programs and also largely absent from English curriculums.

A teaching colleague said recently, "One of the most common complaints I hear from students is that the works they read for English courses are too 'depressing,' and they want to know why we can't read upbeat, 'fun' works." Seth Clabough, who teaches at Sweet Briar College, said his students claim even "happy-*sounding*" works are really about heartaches and they wonder whether a creative work has to be a downer just to qualify for literary merit. "The truth is," Clabough confides, "I am increasingly beginning to wonder, as David Hare recently put it, if the two most depressing words in the English language are 'literary fiction.'"

Dysfunction/pain/loss as themes seem to signal a piece of fiction is at least realistic. Just recently a student turned in the first five chapters of her young adult novel. It was about a fresh-faced teenage girl who adores her adoring parents and loves her life. She is whisked through a wormhole in the space-time continuum where she confronts pirates from another century via an energy anomaly. I knew readers would scoff. "Loves her *parents*? Loves her *life?* Who's going to believe that?"

Setting the Stage

Humor comes from the inside out—like integrity, charisma, and really cool dance moves. And in writing humor, timing is everything, which brings us to Cecelia.

Cecelia was the 3-year-old daughter of a friend and was participating in her preschool's talent night. Ten little girls dressed as fairies had memorized a short dance, spinning in pink tutus, arms curved sweetly in front of them.

A group of boys performed a tumbling act just ahead of the sprites, and as the girls watched from backstage, Cecelia, who had never seen gymnastics before, was enthralled. The girls' music began and nine little fairies began their entrance, tiptoeing onstage to the delicate plinking of violins. Behind them the curtain bumped, bulged, and was suddenly slapped aside as an exuberant Cecelia rolled onto stage as if bowled there. All memory of the dance she'd rehearsed was obliterated. She somersaulted and flapped her way through the performance as the other fairies shuffled tearfully out of her way.

Cecelia demonstrated that when effort follows quickly on the heels of inspiration, we come closest to emulating that which we admire. For writers it is the voice to which we've been most recently exposed, which is why reading humor is the single best method for learning to write humor and the best way to find your humorist's voice. Inundate yourself with the funniest newspaper columns, magazine articles, commentary, and books you can find so you can internalize the pacing, nuances, and candor that create it. Humor is so powerful, however, that it is worth examining its component parts.

When writing reveals that a personal secret is a universal experience, we get to laugh at ourselves in good, if imagined, company. *It's not just me!* you think, a bit giddy with your newfound camaraderie. But the first irony of writing humor is that the stories that make us laugh leave us a bit wistful as well. The ring of laughter resonates with relief and recognition—as if finally you have found your tribe. But discovering your tribe makes you suddenly aware that you have missed them.

The second irony is that if you seek humor it will elude you. Like the constellation Pleiades, which you can usually see in your peripheral vision but that perversely disappears when you try to gaze directly at it. Humor is a by-product of honesty, so put your sights on honesty and allow humor to materialize peripherally.

How? If you hope to write something funny, don't tell a joke, tell a story. And don't just tell what happened. Tell how you felt when

that thing happened. Bare-bones truth-telling takes some real exca-
vation and acute self-awareness. It can also be scary. We might not
look good. Our admissions might make us unlikeable. We might
tumble when we intended to dance. To write humor you have to be
both acutely conscious of self and willing to expose that self.

Self-Exposure

Seinfeld, one of the most successful television sitcoms ever conceived, was based on the principle that almost anything you observe
in your daily life can be funny if you are truthful enough in your
commentary. Just like Michel de Montaigne, father of the essay,
demonstrated, no subject is too mundane. So to write something
funny, you, like the writer of a good sitcom, observe what's around
you, then answer the question, "What's the truth about this?" The
first response to that question is likely to be cliché or superficial,
so you need to ask it again. Then again. Each time you ask, you get
closer to what's true for all of us.

One episode of *Seinfeld*, for instance, involved a character wanting to be seen putting money into a tip jar. When no one witnessed
his act of altruism, he tried to get the money back out to do it again,
in hopes of being acknowledged the second time. Instead he was
accused of stealing from the jar. It was funny because it acted out a
privately harbored, universal desire. We want our altruism noted,
and not by God, for heaven's sake; by the barista who's going to
make our café latte.

David Sedaris, one of our most successful contemporary humor-
ists, is a master at this as well. In recounting the emotional truth of
his very personal experiences, he often hits a chord that resonates.
For instance, in "The Learning Curve" from *Me Talk Pretty One
Day*, Sedaris rehearses ways in which to introduce himself as the
professor to his first writing class. He wants to convey an authority
and expertise he doesn't remotely possess. He wants to sound wise

and professorial, but when the moment comes, he clenches. "In a voice reflecting doubt, fear, and an unmistakable desire to be loved, I sounded not like a thoughtful college professor but, rather, like a high-strung twelve-year-old girl; someone named Brittany."

Although few teachers would articulate this, most of us want to be loved, or at least liked. And broadening the audience, in reality, doesn't everyone? So to have this foible acknowledged is connecting. It exposes the secret we've been harboring and we can laugh along with those fraternal twins: *It's not just me!* and *I'm not crazy!*

Your reader will never laugh because you tell him something is funny. You have to re-create the experience itself and let him draw his own conclusion. Show with details, make them sensory, and be accurate. Don't say "smile," if when you feel into it, that smile was a grimace or too weak to qualify. And look for the humor off-stage from the main action, which is often the source of greatest laughter. For instance, while two women are comically struggling to get the factory-bolted lug nuts off a flat tire so they can change it on the side of the road, the real source of comedy may be what is going on between their kids in the backseat of the car.

Finding What Is Funny

To find a subject, try making a list of the things that drive you nuts, or enlist help by asking your friends about their pet peeves, but be careful. I have a friend whose pet peeve is rich people. She just dislikes them on principle, whereas I think they're fine. But how about people who butt in line like they don't know that's what they've done? The sudden absorption in their cell phones, the lack of eye contact? Or worse, the ones who chat you up. "Hey. How's it going?" forcing you to respond, so that you're now complicit in their rudeness. Is that what's funny? Maybe. It's the first thing that comes to mind.

But if you go deeper, is the greater truth that you are a little afraid of the line-butter? His aggression, his audacity, his willingness to break the rules? You were line leader in elementary school. You love deli counters: Take a number! You want to challenge the offender, but you're nervous, so nonconfrontational that like the line-butter himself you can only take an indirect approach; commenting to "yourself" on the rudeness of "people." Maybe you add to it your best nonverbal reprimand with a look of lethal disapproval—like Bill Bryson's "thundervision."

Exaggeration is another element of humor. So maybe now the line-butter's nonacknowledgment of his crime and your nonac-knowledgment of your annoyance are taking on absurdist propor-tions. Like when the acerbic book critic Anders in Tobias Wolff's short story "Bullet in the Brain" reveals his contempt for the women in line ahead of him, who are complaining that the bank teller has abruptly closed her window. "Damned unfair," he said. "Tragic, really. If they're not chopping off the wrong leg, or bombing your ancestral village, they're closing their position." Funny is usually about a misunderstanding and often exposes a vulnerability. I always feel pretty exposed, for instance, at cosmetic counters. I don't feel pretty, I'm too self-conscious, and I don't want other people to know I care what I look like.

But the other day I got sucked in. I was in pursuit of $65 worth of "free" makeup, my gift for buying $37.50 worth of anything else this national brand was selling. When the makeup girl asked me what I normally use, I actually had no idea, but I did know it was not her brand, which felt like I was being forced to admit I fool around. Like I'd been dating MAC but meeting Bobby Brown for drinks. Buying liquid foundation would qualify for the free stuff, but I had no idea what color to choose.

"Sit," she said, and began daubing my left cheek with something called Buff. I had been clutching my purse, trying not to get seduced into a makeover and now edged one noncommittal hip onto a stool. "Do you have any makeup on?" she asked, switching from Q-tip to sponge.

Shouldn't she know?

She examined my Buff cheek with a critical eye and began sponging Ivory foundation on the other jaw. It was weirdly intimate and I didn't know where to look while the lady worked on my face. Certainly not at *her* face, and not at the cluster of women gathering behind her. Shoppers with time on their hands had slowed to watch like cows bunching up at the barn. I felt guilty—as if I were part of an elaborate con. The herd shifted with what I imagined was disapproval: "Thinks she can *fool* us." "Like *that's* going to help."

Then the consultant held up a mirror and asked me to choose between Buff and Ivory, except that there *was* no difference. Zilch. That was awkward, but I didn't want to hurt her feelings so we both pretended there was, and pretty soon, even the bystanders were weighing in. The free gift bag sat just out of reach on the counter.

"Marlene!" the makeup lady suddenly called out. "Can you come over here, please?" Now we were recruiting the manager for a consult. I was starting to get hot and wished I'd taken my coat off. I smiled hopefully in the direction of the crowd, as if we were friends. We were not. A shadow loomed. Marlene was tall, flawlessly made up, and clearly a man. A very beautiful man. Prettier than I could ever hope to be. The shoppers who'd been observing stirred at the new development.

Marlene stared at me and I gazed anxiously over his head awaiting judgment. He scrutinized my face as if he was sure he'd seen it on a wanted poster, or maybe he was as uncomfortable as I was with the artifice of our dilemma. Marlene gazed in silence so long I thought maybe he was going to say, "The tribe has spoken" and I'd have to leave Makeup Island; no Buff, no Ivory, no free stuff.

"That one," he finally said, pointing at my left cheek with a lovely hand. "And tell her to layer it," he added, releasing me from scrutiny with some free advice.

Writing humor is more about *re*actions than actions. It is more about feelings than events, so you have to figure out how you feel and why, which takes a lot of personal scrutiny and, sometimes, public exposure.

Notice details you think no one else notices. Was the kid with the cold actually depositing something *in*to the salad bar? Try writing out an observation you've had, then tightening it up. Humor cannot afford padding, nor one wasted or misplaced word. Keep it short. Keep it simple. Don't explain the humor. And allow yourself to be surprised. Funny is in the unpredictable. As in Joel Achenbach's essay "Homeward Bound": "My single friends are searching for true love. They are starting to worry. The talent pool is dwindling. I try to be encouraging and offer helpful advice. What I always say is this: 'Start mashing the panic button immediately.'"

Write about family traditions with all their eccentricities, or a relative's quirks. Write about a sibling and re-create your world: the secret code you used; the pet funerals, like Patrick Madden did; the strange rituals. Make a list of all the lies you've ever been told and how you learned the truth, and how something in your life now is bringing the memory to mind.

Make a list of the most embarrassing things that you have ever believed, or that have happened to you, then go deeper and ask yourself what the real humiliation was.

Write about *what transformed* the most disappointing gift you've ever received or given. Write about the one moment you wish you could erase from your past. But keep these things small. Singularities. Stick with one moment—one incident, one exchange in one relationship, one holiday.

Using Humor Wisely

The writing of humor is a delicate skill. It is given birth by letting go of ego, by keen observation, by telling the truth, by acknowledging your own foibles, and by letting the reader make the connection himself to his own failings. Puns are clever, but clever is not the same as funny. And I would never tell a humorous story that relied on a prejudice.

How do you know whether you are being mean or funny? Check in with how you feel when you write something you intend to be humorous. If you feel smart, you may have been condescending. If you feel vindicated, chances are what you have written has a mean-spirited edge. It's like this: I can say some pretty risky things to another person if what I feel is genuine affection, but I can say the most loving things in the world, and if what I'm feeling is satisfied, critical, or *right*, it would be best not to speak. In humor, attitude is everything.

It isn't just what you tell but how you tell it. Humor is a confession, an admission, a conviction of self, and as all those students of literature have observed, we need more of it.

Observe. Explore. Reveal.

Seriously. You'll be funny.

16

Before You Submit:
A Craft Checklist

"Nothing is stopping you from changing the world."
—Noah Lukeman

"Five Tips to Get Published!" "Ten Ways to Plot a Story!" "Six Reasons to Write Your Cat's Memoir!" Succinct and to the point, itemized advice sounds distilled and organized—like there's not going to be a lot of instruction involved.

So here is a submission checklist. Review the following suggestions before you submit work in order to polish your final product:

1. Vary your sentence length. Be sure you have given the work pacing and variety. Remember that an entire sentence can be two words: "She left." "He won." Or three: "My brother lied." And five or six words can foretell a whole plot: "My brother lied to save me." Break up long text into shorter paragraphs to vary them. A paragraph can be comprised of one sentence for effect.

2. Delete your adjectives. Go back through your work, pulling out the adjectives and adverbs on one test page. Now read it over and see if it doesn't sound more professionally written. We get lazy with adjectives and tend to line them up and ask them to do our showing for us. Never send in an adjective when what you need is a verb.

3. Excise the excess. Don't use two similes in a sentence if one does the job sufficiently. Don't explain what you've just shown. I'll stop there.

4. Check your weight limit. Review your major themes, plots, and characters in terms of time onstage. Is there too much of one and not enough of another? Are they too evenly weighted or disproportionate for their roles?

5. Authenticity. Are people dressed as they should be for the weather? For their time period? Check newspaper archives, or the Sears Roebuck catalog from the last century. For speech patterns and word usage, check the *Dictionary of American Slang* or the *Oxford English Dictionary* for the first appearance of terms. Review old maps in order to refer to regions and places by their historically correct references. Think about the environment: What form of lighting was common? Kerosene lamps? Candles? Rag torches? Investigate customs: Were widows informed of war casualties, or did they have to consult newspaper listings? Married at 12, at what age did royal spouses actually cohabitate?

Are children acting, thinking, and speaking like children, not miniature adults? Does time pass? Is someone too good? Is a place too clean? Did you remember to use masculine similes for male characters and feminine similes for your female characters when appropriate? "Running was his talent, like some guys are born with a pitcher's arm."

6. Setting. Did you include one? Is it the right one? Yes, but more than one? Does time pass in your setting? Do seasons pass? Does your setting underscore the emotional content of each scene?

7. Replace description with action. Have you used description to tell something you should have shown?

8. Read aloud. Read to someone else. Cut all the pages you find yourself reading quickly or stopping to summarize in order to skip.

Check your syntax. How does the work sound? Does it flow? Are you suddenly aware of repeated words?

9. Add simile and metaphor. Contrasting two unlike objects can illuminate a third object in a brilliantly original way that makes us see it more clearly. Look through your manuscript at places you have made a statement that could be illuminated with a simile: "The house was hot." True, but "the house was as hot as a locked car in a Florida theme park" may be better.

10. Reframe negative descriptions as positives. Positive descriptions are easier for our brains to decode and are usually a more simplistic grammatical construction. Describe an object in terms of what it is, not what it isn't.

11. Use the printer. Be flagrant in your use of the printer. This is a place to spend money even though ink is costly. But as you revise and cut and paste material, you simply must clear the decks of the old and see it fresh and new. Print out new versions, bundle the old, and file them away for a while.

12. Steal from yourself. You may have an unpublished essay somewhere with a perfect description you could lift and add to your novel. For example, I plan to steal this from myself someday:

> *When I can't get an appointment with the psychotherapist I call the psychic. Why examine the past, if my fate is in the cards?*

13. Create a great lines file. Some of your most original similes, evocative descriptions, and heart-piercing dialogue may not enhance your story as a whole. Sometimes our best writing, just like our weakest, is drawing attention to itself. Create a great lines folder; cut the lines but place them there. Use the file for inspiration as needed. The paragraph you had to sacrifice because it overpowered the original piece can be the nucleus of a new piece or useful elsewhere.

14. Check for cause/effect. Do things flow in a way that makes sense? No dangling loose ends? No jumps in logic or time that require a transition? Speaking of which, are your transitions smooth? Can you add a double space to clarify a scene change, or add a sentence or two? Begin a new chapter? Add asterisks for a graphic transition?

15. Set the work aside. A couple of hours, a couple of days, a couple of weeks will be even better. Let your mind reboot.

16. Read someone you admire. Then pick up your work again. Read an author whose voice greatly differs from your own.

17. Ask for help. Ask for the kind of help you want. Ask experts.

18. Go on a cliché hunt. Be ruthless. Ferret them out.

19. Swap out weak verbs for stronger ones. Original verbs. Tell your nouns to get off the couch and act like verbs, like Ron Hansen does so beautifully in *Mariette in Ecstasy*. Example: a young novice hangs wet sheets on a clothesline until she is "curtained" and "roomed" by them.

20. Get creative with structure. Try cutting your first or last paragraph, first or last page. Try swapping the positions of your last and first paragraphs. You may find a new structure that makes the whole story suddenly original. Begin with the end. Tell the entire story backward. Open with the crises you embedded in the middle.

21. Pretend you are someone else. Read your story as if you are the editor to whom you want to send it, or a friend. Read the piece listening for their perspective. Would they think your description was over the top? Would they be bored with the lengthy psychological backstory you included?

22. Retype your entire essay or story. Just re-enter it in your computer, keystroke for keystroke. Invariably you improve the work yet again.

23. Check character names. Do they work for you? Is your bank robber named "Chase"? Is your philandering husband John Strayfield? Without sliding into cartoon mode, think about what your character names evoke on a subliminal level.

24. Make your stakes clear. Does the reader know who stands to lose what and how much it means? Is there a marriage at stake? A life? A person's integrity? A job? A political party?

25. Check your ending. If you read just the last page, do you still like your ending? Try reading just the last two paragraphs of every story in an anthology. Amazingly, many of the great ones are interesting, moving, or entertaining, *even when you haven't read the rest of the story.* Identify the ones you like the best and see what the author did that you can apply to your own ending.

26. Clean up your office. Sometimes you need to take a break from the work without getting too far away from it. The work in your head has become so intense or a plot so complex that you need the physical space around you to be spare and clean. Declutter your environment. Wipe off surfaces, put your books back on the shelf, refill the printer. Throw out all those scraps of paper with ideas on them that you have now used. Take any work or folders that you are not currently using out of play by boxing them up and storing them (labeled) for another time.

27. Submit. Keep your motivation high with the possibility of publication. No one is going to come find you in your foxhole. Send work out on a rotating basis so that something is always in play.

Part 3

Spirit: Caring for the Writer

17

Time and Writing with Children

P. G. Wodehouse is said to have dedicated a novel to his young children, "without whose constant love and affection this book would have been finished in half the time."

I once heard Tom Clancy speak at a writers' association meeting. *The Hunt for Red October,* which he had written while selling insurance, had just been published. It was his "debut" novel and a blockbuster. He was not young. Illuminated by the stage lights, Clancy looked out over legions of hopefuls seated in the dark and said, "Just write the damn book." As he continued to share his experience, he'd interrupt himself or pause to admonish us again: "Write the damn book." All that lost time, Clancy was telling us, when he could have been a best-selling author. His message was clear: Kids or no kids. Job or no job. Time or no time. It is never too late and never too early to embrace the dream.

I thought of this as my fiction class gathered the other afternoon. I have a couple of boys from the community college in that class, a retired journalist, and two middle-aged women writing young adult novels, but Cheryl is the only writer in the mix with a preschool child, and she came in looking strange.

Her normally silky dark hair was hanging limp on her shoulders and her skin looked gray. At one point while we were discussing similes her eyelids fluttered closed, snapped open, closed again, then opened halfway, like someone inside her head was playing with the blinds. She lasted until the break, then left. Later that night I received an e-mail:

> *Sorry about class. I'm pregnant. Believe it or not, I went home, ate waffles, and felt so much better. It's twins. I was sick tonight, but writing feels farther and farther away the more real this becomes. How am I going to keep my writing alive with three little ones? What expectations and goals should I have during these years?*

Expectations? Low ones. Goals? Not a good word, although Seth Clabough, the instructor at Sweet Briar whose students were bemoaning "downer-based fiction," has four kids under the age of 7, has a wife who works as well, and is writing a novel. He says having limited time can be an advantage because it forces him to be more productive.

I know of a mother who wrote her first book hiding from her kids in the family van. It was parked in the driveway and stocked with animal crackers. And of another who wrote her first book in her bedroom closet with a flashlight. When my kids were small, the house was quiet. I could write while they napped or before they got up in the morning. Then they grew big and loud. They got lacrosse sticks and violins. They used them in the house. For writers who are parents, for writers who work at home, for writers who need to carve their writing life out of a larger, intense priority, like a full-time job, there are remedies for interruptions, lack of time, and privacy.

Remedies

Drag a desk into any small useless room and call it your study. Make it off limits. Swap out the solid wood door for a glass-paned French door, so you are there but not there, sort of like working in the garden means you're home, but not *in-the-house* home. Children or a spouse can come to the door of your study in an emergency, but they can't come in. You may find, however, that someone pantomiming needs on the other side of the glass is as distracting as someone who simply walks in to search for the channel changer. So wean yourself from reacting to interruptions until you can observe a family member gesticulating on the other side of the door dispassionately, as if you are teammates in a game of charades. Flailing arms, eyebrows raised in alarm, could mean anything—*Flood in the basement! Intruder in the kitchen!* Keep writing the damn book.

After space, go for privacy—a password on your computer, then a password on the screen saver. Try having zero expectations. I say *try* because expectations will probably seep through your best intentions like sound seeps through those earphones that make white noise. Try getting out of the house to bond with other writers in cafés, although this requires the expense of sitters, which will not be as expensive as the coffee. Try to combine worlds by taking work along to the park and the pool, where you'll stare into space and not write anything. Call this "percolating."

No one else in these places will have brought a laptop because good parents put their children first. They willingly focus on swim team, play practices, and play dates, and these are super-smart, accomplished, selfless parents who can balance checkbooks *and* think about others. Keep working on that *me*-moir. These same people give to the community, but you're not a joiner. You don't want to be Room Mother or Scout Leader or serve on the Civic Association. Try to comprehend the unfathomable debt you owe to those who do.

At least you can be *responsible*. You can show up on time for everything; it's just that you'll often be thinking about something you want to write, sometimes making notes to yourself while you wait for the kids in the car. When they climb into the backseat, you'll be laughing at something you've written and forget to ask how their day was. Or you'll be teary, which will make the children exchange worried glances and then stare out the windows.

You will hear about this 20 years from now in the first family session of their therapy. That's the session where the therapist asks you to join them. Then he's seen all he needs to see, only you don't know what it was, and he doesn't ask you to come back. Write about him.

You could arrange play dates to give yourself breaks in which to write, but then you'd have to have other people's children over and you don't really like other people's children. Don't admit this. Ever. No one will forgive it. Even you.

Eventually you will learn like other writers before you that when retreat doesn't work, one way to simultaneously parent and hang on to your identity as a writer is by surrendering to the chaos. Record these years; observe them; take some notes.

Just Take Notes

Brian Doyle is not just a writer but the full-time editor of *Portland Magazine* and the father of three. Finding time to write or do anything that nurtures himself as an individual isn't easy. Like basketball. Doyle played from grade school through college and beyond. It was part of his well-being and an activity he enjoyed with great gusto, but:

> *I got hurt, everyone does eventually; I got hurt enough to quit. ... The game receded, fell away, a part of me sliding into the dark like a rocket stage no longer part of the mission.*

Putting your writing aside can feel like that—like whole huge chunks of yourself have fallen away—which is why so many people struggle to hang on to this part, this writer self, by whatever means possible.

So when Doyle could no longer play pickup basketball in the park, he made teammates of his then 4-year-old daughter Lily and 1-year-old twins, Liam and Joe. He writes in the breathless prose of an athlete in action, of a writer who needs to write, of a parent who wants to remember:

> Yesterday my daughter and I played two on two against my sons on the lovely burnished oak floor of our dining room, the boys who just learned to walk staggering across the floor like drunken sailors and falling at the slightest touch, my daughter loud lanky in her orange socks sliding from place to place without benefit of a dribble but there is no referee only me on my knees, dribbling behind my back and trick-dribbling through the plump legs of the boys, their diapers sagging, my daughter shrieking with glee, the boys confused and excited, and I am weeping, weeping, weeping, in love with my hands, my arms at home in the old motions, my head and shoulders snapping fakes on the boys, who laugh.

I want to share all of this with my student Cheryl: the empathy of wanting to hang on to that inner identity and the joy of what is to come even if she loses herself for a while. The truth is I no longer know whether I'd even advise trying to cling to the old model. I clung so hard to that separate self in order to have one when the kids left because I thought it was insurance against the sadness of letting them go. It wasn't. I wanted them to be proud of me for being something other than their mother when being their mother would have been enough. I also think my writing probably felt intrusive.

But then there is this: the essays you write and publish during their baby and elementary school years and even high school years (by then it will have to be fiction) are documentation, in a way, of how much you loved them because things get lost over time—or doubted. And those moments where they made you helpless with laughter or brought you to your knees might be forgotten by you and a revelation to them.

Well into his two-on-two pickup basketball game in the dining room, Doyle continues in the voice of a sports announcer:

... but here comes big Liam, lumbering along toward the ball as alluring and bright as the sun; crossover dribble back to my right hand, Liam drops like a stone, he spins on his bottom to stay with the play, I palm ball, show fake, and lean into short fallaway from 4 feet away, ball hits rim of basket and bounces straight up in the air, Lily slides back into picture and grabs my right hand but I lean east and with the left hand catch and slam the ball into the basket all in one motion; and it bounces off a purple plastic duck and rolls away under the table, and I lie there on the floor as Joe pulls on my sock and Lily sits on my chest and Liam ever so gently, so meticulously, so daintily takes off my glasses, and I am happier than I have ever been, ever and ever, amen.

Time as Ally

My mother is 90 and the possessor of all our family history. The sepia photos of a long-lost family farm, black-and-white pictures of my grandparents posing by their spanking new model T Ford as if it had no more significance than a tree stump. (Facial expressions apparently evolved sometime around 1956.) If my mother doesn't label these photos soon, their meaning will be lost. "We had a boat named *Windfall*?" she asks. She looks at me as if this fact is a puzzle she must solve. If she is forgetting, I will forget. You will forget.

So get it all down now even if you don't know what you are going to do with it. Capture on paper the first time you heard your son laugh, your parents harmonize to "Moon River," the smell of a dog who has rolled on a dead fish. But don't wait.

Write the damn book.

18

Using Intuition to
Guide Your Work

*"It is my belief that as writers we, too, often access information
beyond our normal realm of knowing."*
—Julia Cameron

*In general terms, I think of intuition as an alertness to what's there.
Most of my stories have started with what I call potent glimpses: a
brief sighting of someone or something that, for mysterious reasons,
snags in my mind and stays there. Months or years later, this image
might surface and become the basis of a story, or two separate images
might collide in my mind and set off a new galaxy of associations.*

According to Barbara Klein Moss, author of *Little Edens*, intuition is
basic to any fiction writer's process. Intuition is part of the mysterious process that brings a story into existence, and it is a resource
you should cultivate. Defined as "instinctive or immediate knowledge," intuition is a way of accessing information not available to
your rational mind. It is inspired creativity. When you hear a writer
say that a story "wrote itself," or that the writer "had no idea that
plot twist was going to happen," you are hearing about intuition
in action. It is almost as if, once we have placed our attention on a
subject, we have simultaneously placed an order with the world at
large to add to our database. Moss continues:

A few summers ago we went to Farnsworth Museum in Rockland,
Maine. I was struck by a painting: a landscape of the village of
Blue Hill, with each of its small buildings carefully detailed, and
in the bottom right corner, a man in a tall hat waving a stick at a
snake, chasing the serpent out of Blue Hill. The artist was Jonathan
Fisher, pastor of the Blue Hill Congregational Church in the late-
eighteenth and early-nineteenth century, a stern Calvinist whose
many talents included inventing his own coded language.

Since I had just started a novel about a New England seminary
student from around the same era, who is obsessed with language,
the painting seemed like a gift. I read a biography of Fisher, and
was so taken with him that I created a character loosely based on
him. He's become an important figure in the novel, and Parson
Fisher is still part of my life. The next summer we went to Blue
Hill to visit the house he built, which still stands, and we've gone
back every summer since.

I'd like to feel the ornery old curmudgeon is sending blessings down
on his fictional alter-ego but more likely he's turning in his grave.
Never mind—last August we went to Blue Hill cemetery and laid
a flower on it anyway.

In Western culture, we have been traditionally taught to suppress
insights in favor of a rational view. We are even taught to associate
intuition with the paranormal: precognitive dreams, telepathy, and
other compelling but only anecdotally verifiable phenomenon. Yet
intuition deserves acknowledgment; it should be cultivated and
practiced just like any other writing skill.

Intuition is, in part, a form of attention that comes from the root
word meaning "reach toward." We mentally reach toward whatever
we are thinking about, concentrating on, or interested in. When I
place my attention on antique cameos because my character pur-
chased a cameo locket at an estate sale, suddenly I begin finding

references to antique jewelry everywhere I look. A magazine in the dentist's waiting room will be left open to a feature on rose cameos. Someone will step into the same elevator wearing an exquisite piece and be willing to talk about its origin. Or perhaps now that cameos are in my mental orbit, I stumble onto a PBS documentary about how they are made.

Allowing Intuition

One way to access intuition is to assume there is significance in the things that pop into your head, especially those inner voices that won't be stilled or those partial melodies that relentlessly repeat themselves. I used to resist. I'd try replacing the annoying repetition of one of those awful songs with the melody to "Happy Birthday" (also awful), or I'd try my husband's morally questionable remedy: off-loading the offending refrain by "sharing" it.

Instead of resisting, stop and listen to the music. Recently I was writing in a local café and found myself debating whether two characters should engage in a dialogue or bury their feelings and move on with their conflict unresolved. I'm a talker, and my character wanted to talk. But I suspected the father in the story needed time and distance. Words were too intense, too overwhelming for him in his grief. The pause felt frustrating and, well, inefficient.

I drove home wrestling with the issue and finally turned on the radio as a distraction. A song I didn't know was playing loudly. I waited for it to end but it seemed to go on forever. When I finally glanced down at the radio in order to change the station, I noticed there was an LED window on the radio displaying the band's name, like the news crawl on television that warns of impending severe thunderstorms. I rarely listen to the car radio and had never noticed it had this capability, but there it was, digitally displayed. The band's name? "Conversation Kills."

So the next time this happens to you, identify the music. If you don't consciously know the title or the lyrics, look them up. You may find your wise subconscious has been rooting through your memory's junk drawer, or through stimulus in your immediate environment, looking for a way to reach you with an insight.

To ignore those messages is like not cashing in a lotto ticket. As novelist Mark Bailey says:

> *Intuition has different meanings to different individuals. To some, it is their guardian angel. To others, it is the universal mind. To others, it may be science not yet discovered. As a writer, primarily of fiction, I depend on this sense of otherness to guide me. I spent two years, a few thousand dollars of my wife's and my hard-earned savings to travel to Italy to research the necropolis beneath the Vatican. It wasn't rational. I just felt a pang in my gut that this was worth doing. The result was my first novel, SAINT.*

Developing Intuition

Intuition comes from a place so deep it must often resort to sign language, but it is in constant conversation with you if you are aware, like the bumper sticker that proclaims "Believe" when you are ready to give up on your writing, like the dump truck tailgate stenciled "Do Not Push" (more advice on same).

Notice what you notice. Billboards, magazine headlines, newspaper articles. Everything. You carry your story with you in your head throughout the day, and it is as if that energy is a beacon. As Julia Cameron says, when a writer places his attention on a topic, he is posing a question to the universe that asks "Do you have information for me about this?" Frequently, according to Cameron, the response is yes, and from a variety of sources.

Once attention is focused on your topic, it will draw to you myriad forms of assistance: books, snippets of conversation, experts,

Internet links, anecdotes, or in Bailey's case, a persistent need to investigate and in Moss's case, art. So ask questions of your inner guidance. What should my character wear? What is the next conflict? What does my character need to know? Insights do come to us unbidden, but formally asking frames the issue and focuses energy on it in a way that enhances vague wondering.

If you are stuck in a story or wrestling with a character, ask yourself what you should do just before meditating or before going to sleep at night. In the morning, write down the first things that pop into your head or simply get to work without interruption.

Try visualizing. Think back to a moment in the past when you have had a major insight. It doesn't have to have been about writing; it can have been an insight about anything. Feel again how you felt then. Remember where you were, the ah-ha sense of suddenly knowing the answer. Now, while feeling those same emotions, imagine receiving an insight about the current conundrum.

Electricity was a natural phenomenon at work long before we recognized and harnessed it. Someday we may look at the use of intuition in much the same way. So suspend your disbelief. Just as we did with creativity, welcome intuition by allowing yourself to believe you possess it—we all do, even if you can't point to any concrete experiences where you are certain intuition played a role.

Make up a one-page vignette where you simply imagine on the page how you figured something out. Just invent it. This is a technique used in hypnosis to get memory and intuition flowing. "I was stuck on how to move from Virginia's near drowning to John's invitation when suddenly I had an insight involving a candle left burning in the bedroom." Again, you are just imagining the arrival of a solution and you can write anything at all, because the act of writing and assuming a solution opens the door so inner guidance can come through. It's the fake-it-till-you-make-it way to generate an insight.

As a writer, I have experienced at least one message that seemed to come from some resource larger than myself. I was working on a novel that felt thin on plot. Still, I loved it enough to continue to invest in it. As a remedy I wanted to include a new character: a visiting professor from New Zealand. In the novel, he joins the faculty of the College of Charleston for a one-year visiting professor's tenure in the English Department. He brings with him a new direction for the book's main character, but I wasn't sure whether it was an inspired addition or an unnecessary tangent I'd regret including.

I flew to Charleston for a week to immerse myself in the setting. I walked brick sidewalks under spreading live oaks draped in Spanish moss, strolled along the Battery—the waterfront park where the city's two great rivers meet—and explored the college campus. Still unsure, on the last day before heading home I decided to visit one of the town's marinas. My visiting professor, if he were included, was going to live on a houseboat while in Charleston, I'd decided.

The day was bright with sunshine; white caps whipped the waves where hundreds and hundreds of boats rocked in slips along the weathered docks. Powerboats were tied next to sailboats, visiting vessels were nestled next to local ones, the bright light of midday bounced blindingly off the white hulls. I walked the maze of piers aimlessly, my doubts and questions ever on my mind, until a J-22, moored stern end to the pier, brought me to a halt.

The vessel's homeport, like most of the others, was the city of Charleston. But her name was the *Kia Ora*, which in New Zealand means "hello."

At home the following week, I wrote my new character onto a flight from Auckland to LAX. A two-hour layover, a five-hour redeye, and he was in Charleston, just where he belonged.

You are companioned by support in any creative project if you just respond to the tap on the shoulder, listen to the music in your head, open the universe's mail.

19

Jealousy: Your Tough-Love Friend

"I feel a lot of guilt about [success]. I can also tell you it unleashes a lot of malice. You pay for your success in many ways—in other writers and other people."
—Margaret Drabble

When a friend told me he'd landed a top agent I heartily congratulated him. When he later complained that the agent wasn't answering his e-mails, I commiserated with him. When he fired the agent, I attaboyed him. When he went directly to a publisher and pulled off a book contract, I celebrated with him. I was happy for my friend. We had soared and plummeted together with the ups and down of our literary endeavors. And there was this: If he can do it, so can I.

But there was also this: He's firing top agents, and I can't even land a crappy one. Hell, I can write better than he can—he's just a better self-promoter and knows how to leverage contacts. Three years from now he'll be negotiating movie rights and I'll be self-published.

I feel guilty about such thoughts. But if circumstances were reversed? He'd probably feel the same about me.

Writer and professor Hank Parker knows when someone else receives a two-book contract based on one essay or an invitation to become a client of a top literary agency, or sells the first short story he's ever written to a literary review you revere, it is only human to feel a moment of envy. Maybe it's more than a moment. Maybe it's an entire crummy day. You have close calls with pedestrians in crosswalks and elevate the dog to his new standing as Best Friend in the Universe.

Maybe your friend's good news makes you wonder why you ever wanted to be a stupid writer. Why you are being denied—which you clearly are—any reward for your equal if not greater effort. Maybe your friend has worked harder and is more talented, but as Parker noted, envy is quick to whisper, *it was a matter of unseemly self-promotion and luck*.

This Is Gonna Hurt ...

The feelings are even more complex when you have had a hand in your friend's success. Linda Woolford, who publishes fiction in top literary reviews, explains the very honest ambivalence.

> *I launch my email, and there, in the subject line, "Woo-Hoo!!!!"* *and the name of some prestigious literary journal. The very journal, that just this morning sent me a form rejection. The email is from one or another member of my writing group, and I know intimately the story that will soon appear in the coveted journal. I've known this story from infancy, have helped raise it to the stunner it currently is.* Congratulations! You are so talented. I'm so happy for you!! *I reply, and I mean every word. But once I hit send, I figure I deserve some downtime, because her news has also left me feeling wretchedly dull and untalented. And a little miffed. That's* the last time I give *her* such thorough critiques, *I think.* Why am I helping her get published? *Such tricky business, literary jealousy, so double-edged.*

Envy is a form of hunger, a form of longing. It's an emotion no one wants to claim. I know. I've asked around. Writers will discuss the intimate details of the struggle to tell the truth, to face their demons on the page. They'll talk about rejection, but to admit feeling envy is pretty unflattering, much like admitting conceit. But remove your judgment of this very natural response and it becomes something else.

Envy is your tough-love friend. It is nothing more than a signal to yourself identifying what you want. I know what you're thinking: *Brilliant insight! I want success!* But if you change the way you look at envy, envy will change the way it looks at you. Instead of regarding you as deficient, *left behind*, and a less-than loser, envy will simply regard you as *informed*. And that's how you'll feel: alerted to a condition that needs addressing.

Put Envy to Work

Maybe you haven't actually been sending material out on a regular basis. Maybe you have been sending out the same stories again and again but not writing something new. Maybe you have not done the research required to send your material to the places most likely to publish it in terms of length, style, and content. Maybe you have been sending things to contests when you should have been sending them through regular submission channels. Envy can be informing you, to your great benefit, of many things you need to know; things that will make you happier, a better caretaker of your craft. How can something so good for you feel so bad?

Because writers have no control; it is one of the few professions in the world in which education, talent, hard work, and perseverance may still not be rewarded. In addition, the personal critic we met in Chapter 1 is quick to make comparisons. Fear will try to reestablish the myth that good fortune, like inspiration, is a limited commodity, and your friend just took your allotment. It's as if you are on a lifeboat and the survivors are passing around a bottle with the last of the water, and your friend, who is about to pass the jug to you, looks you square in the eye and chugs down your portion. Not only is that unfair and you were unprepared, but you know *it's never going to rain again and you're never going to be rescued.*

Envy sends us reeling into infantile thinking—words like "never" and "always" are its hallmarks. "I'll *never* get published." "He *always* wins everything." One moment, one event, becomes all that will ever be.

When my youngest daughter Emily was a baby, we needed a break, and though I was reluctant to leave her, we asked my mother to come stay with her overnight and farmed the older kids out to friends. Emily couldn't talk yet, but I told her goodbye and that we loved her (because babies, like dogs, understand everything you say) and off we went to what had appeared to be a charming Bed and Breakfast within a four-hour drive of home. Note to self: Use Google Earth next time you choose a Bed and Breakfast on the Internet to avoid gas station and creepy graveyard 3 feet out of camera range.

We were only going to be gone 24 hours, but I didn't realize that Emily was living on infant time—the present was eternity. She stopped eating, cried inconsolably, and refused to sleep. She *grieved.* Her mother and father had said goodbye and disappeared, and it was forever.

When you feel the pain of envy, which is not unlike the pain of abandonment, remember that it comes from a very young place inside—an immature place where conditions that are only momentary feel permanent.

Antidotes

When your friend says he has just been accepted as a client of a prominent literary agency, you say, "Great!" but what you think is, "Wait! They should know about me! If they like you, they'll like me. Maybe they'll like me *because* they like you!" Once again it feels as if success is not a renewable resource. Ridiculous.

There is one guaranteed antidote to jealousy: creativity.

Get back to your own work. Go back to the page. Getting back into your own creative project will reestablish your equilibrium by connecting you to yourself again, pulling you back in where you belong instead of hanging out in the empty isolation of another's success. And remember, creativity is not simply being busy. It means making something.

Reconnecting with yourself by creating something new fills you up so that your congratulations are not only genuine, they bring you home to yourself again. Write another paragraph, another page. Start a new story. Get out some of your best work and reread it. Change a few lines. Send it out to three places you haven't tried, then rearrange your furniture. Replace the green placemats with the blue ones. Change your energy. Go out and work in the garden to connect yourself to the earth. Go for a walk or a run so that exercise endorphins will allow you to leapfrog over the wall you've built around your misery. Envy is distorting. It is a thief. It makes you forget who you really are.

Think of the publishing world as a huge, gaping maw that must be fed copious amounts of new material today, tomorrow, and every single day beyond that. Every time a manuscript is accepted, the editor is looking ahead to fill next month's or next year's void. Think of the publishing world's needs as infinite. You need to understand,

deep in your soul, that new opportunities to publish replace every
single accepted manuscript. Barbara Kingsolver writes:

> This manuscript of yours that has just come back from another
> editor is a precious package. Don't consider it rejected. Consider that
> you've addressed it "to the editor who can appreciate my work" and
> it has simply come back stamped "not at this address." Just keep
> looking for the right address.

Envy can be a prison. Ironically, you are the judge, jury, and jailor
who put yourself there, and the whole prison exists in your head. So
keep your perspective, because the mind can be a dangerous place
to wander around in alone. Get out and do something for someone
else—and that's *after* you have actually taken a shower and put on
some decent clothes. I know you are never going to see anyone else
again *ever*, and nothing really matters anymore, so what's the point,
but pretend. Call someone you've neglected, give up a parking
space, smile and thank a surly sales clerk even though you'd like to
kick something (probably her).

Practice the art of detachment. Imagine, just for today, that what
you are writing matters and that it has a purpose in this world even
if you can't see that success realized at this time. How would that
change your feelings of envy? How would it change what you write?
It really is the *creation* of the work that has value to you, that ener-
gizes your life, and that gives you a means to express your singular
self. Emily Dickinson wrote over 1,700 poems, yet actively avoided
publication. Only seven pieces of verse saw print in her lifetime.
The purpose was in the writing. This is hard for us to remember
and for others to understand. Helen Hunt Jackson is said to have
reprimanded Dickinson, "It is a wrong to the day you live in, that
you will not sing aloud." But Dickinson was doing what she loved in
the way that served her best.

Remind yourself as well that you do not know good news from
bad. Part of your envy is fueled by your assumption that someone

else's success is a wonderful experience for them when in fact you have no idea what pressures, disappointments, failed expectations, and mistakes may be playing out.

Regain your sense of humor. I would like to be as well published as my friend Brian Doyle, whose work has appeared in these pages. When that sense of longing starts to materialize, I remind myself that Brian would simply like to have his name spelled correctly. In his role as writer and editor, he has been referred to as Drain Boyle, Brain Doyle, Byron Dhyle, and Brian Dooley. I smile every time I think of this. It reminds me that I like Brian. Goodwill brings me home to myself.

Along with humor, get some perspective. There are people out there with real problems, and you probably know a few of them. Remind yourself of the things for which you are truly grateful. Write them down, and don't be piddly about it. You cannot feel gratitude and envy at the same time. It is impossible.

Make a plan of action. Plans are liberating; plans are fuel; plans are hope. They organize our longing and give it tools. They refocus the energy of our desire.

What's true, as Woolford says, is that embedded in virtually every exuberant announcement of an acceptance is the sentiment:

And the next woo-hoo message to go out may be yours! *The likeliness of this helps me regain enough of a sense of balance to realize that there's value in the struggle. Value in honoring the snarled, jangly feelings of envy, and giving them some space, and value in struggling to let those feelings go and to embrace happiness for the triumphant friend. Value in knowing the messy, complicated struggle is human. And certainly value if I can use this knowledge in creating ever more complex and nuanced fiction. I am happy for my writer friend, even if it hurts, and this leads me to email her, P.S.* Hey, let's get together soon and open a bottle of champagne.

20
Choosing Your Genre

"It is time to get a new map or revise the one you have."
—Sanaya Roman

I will never make the choice between writing fiction or nonfiction because I still don't understand the distinction. I don't think nonfiction even exists. I just never thought about it that way. I thought fiction meant the lines went to the end of the page. I never thought for five minutes that fiction meant you made stuff up.

Pam Houston, a well-published short story writer who frequently publishes nonfiction as well, was explaining her experience with the fiction versus nonfiction conundrum at an annual writers' convention. The admission generated a short wave of relieved applause. You could almost hear the audience thinking, "Hey! She's successful at both genres and even *she's* confused." It was a lot like getting a glimpse of a classmate's grade and discovering the smartest kid in school also got the essay question wrong. The audience also appeared grateful for the author's candor. As she spoke, outright laughter was followed by several more waves of applause.

If you have been struggling with your choice of genre, with the distinctions between fiction and nonfiction, it's time to experiment, to embrace the genre of your natural voice, and to lay the burden of ambiguity down.

Fiction and nonfiction are like friends with emotional boundary issues. Of course we know nonfiction means "this is real," and fiction means "I made this up," but neither genre is ever quite that pure. It is hard to know where one leaves off and the other begins. Houston's short story collection, *Cowboys Are My Weakness,* is full of romantic adventures had by a young woman (not her …) who is attracted to a certain kind of alpha male. When it was published, readers wanted to know how much of the stories were true. In exasperation, Houston finally picked an arbitrary number: *Eighty-two percent of my fiction is really about me, okay?* Later, when she published a book of essays, her fans felt they had flushed her out. "Gotcha," they seemed to say. They finally had 100 percent. Uh, no, the author told them. Somehow, even in nonfiction, what was real still came out to about 82 percent.

Despite the actual relationships or events that ignite a story, the moment it becomes language it is changed. Here, once again, the world of science and art collide. We have discovered on a quantum level that simply observing an event affects its outcome. The minute you put pen to paper, what happened becomes something else and the real people in your life become, on some level, characters.

Several other writers who publish successfully in multiple genres were also speaking at this conference, sharing their struggles with black-and-white definitions. Another panelist wrote a series of short stories that were consistently mistaken for memoir. Then he published a memoir people referred to as a novel.

> *Everything I write starts out in nonfiction in my mind, because I don't have a holiday-making spirit, but for me fiction is not about disguising what happened, it's about creating drama.*

Another panelist seemed to feel that nonfiction is the truth, while fiction has the seed of truth.

The truth versus fiction can be really painful when it comes to reviews, said a petite, pretty author also on the panel. When her first book, a novel about a promiscuous girl, was published, it was very favorably received. But when her memoir was published and covered the same material, she was vilified. Critics called her names, and not the nice ones. It was traumatizing. Humiliating. Sharing the ordeal with a sympathetic audience, however, was therapeutic. "Guess I'm still working it through," she laughed, looking small and vulnerable.

The panelists continued to speak candidly about the overlaps, constraints and possibilities of writing in multiple genres, and, specifically, moving between fiction and nonfiction without feeling squeamish. In an industry where it is hard to tell fact from fiction anymore, one writer said bookstores might as well label genre sections "Fictionish," "Memoirish," and "Cartoonish."

When Changing Genres Means Changing Forms

A few years ago I switched genres. I was publishing personal essays about parenthood, about those moments when you know you would step in front of a train to protect your child; those moments that exist only in your anxiety-prone imagination, however, because life is going to exact much less dramatic ways to prove your love, like removing spiders from beneath bike seats in a dark garage.

But I wasn't writing about sex, temptation, betrayal, and deceit. I felt, like so many writers, that fiction might allow the latitude of more compelling conflicts. At least it would afford more commercially viable conflicts. If you write essay, it sometimes feels as if fiction is the glamour girl who lives in New York City and you are hanging out in the 'burbs with nonfiction, her loser friend from middle school. Yes, fiction would make my work multidimensional. I'd switch genres.

At first it was a struggle to use imagination more than memory. Using anything autobiographical felt like cheating—as if I might be exposed and arrested by the fiction police. This is a common insecurity when switching from nonfiction to fiction, and like many fiction novices and all the panelists, all my early short stories began with some nugget of truth. The last gesture of a dying friend who could no longer speak I gave to a character whose estranged father had never once voiced his love. He gathers her hand to his heart and holds it there, as if pulling her inside him or making a sacred vow.

I gave the incident of getting my first speeding ticket to a character who has been ticketed 19 times in the two weeks since her boyfriend left her. I began to worry less and have fun. I began to love these stories, and it was true that fiction was a marvelous way to tell multifaceted truths. I published a little. My work was accepted by an experienced and generous agent in New York ... and that's when the trouble began. I discovered that if fiction is more glamorous than nonfiction, a novel is the truly hot commodity.

Writing to Sell

Collections are rarely published by unknown writers. Write a novel, the agent said, and we'll submit both simultaneously. A novel was as far from the essays of my early work as a marathon is from a jog around the block, but I wanted a book. New York wants a novel? All-righty then. Coming right up. No matter that the form was less natural to me; no matter that novel writing takes years and you basically have to teach yourself. If those publishers had suggested I swing a dead cat from a string at midnight, I'd have probably been crouched in the backyard with a ball of twine calling the cat.

So I wrote a novel based on a short story called *Point of Impact*. It was, indeed, based upon a nugget of truth—my childhood—in which bad things happened to small people. I didn't so much have a story to tell as a story to *sell*. This was a huge mistake. You can't try to make a story interesting at the expense of being *interested* in the telling. It was a bad book with some passable writing in it. I liked the title.

I wrote a second book in which good people do bad things. I can't remember the title. I began a third novel based on a frivolous lawsuit to which my husband and I had been subjected. I titled it *Adverse Possession*, which refers to a property law that says what you own but don't use, you lose—only my book was about a marriage. *Get it?* My agent thought it was thin on plot. "You need a hook," she said, "Give me something to sell." Not to worry. I made my characters descendants of nefarious pirates. I added a tribe of mystical warriors, secret identities, and a death.

Here, kitty.

But when I awoke in the mornings and went to my desk, the writing was something to figure out, a calculation to be completed. Aspiration had overcome inspiration, and I felt more like a contortionist than a writer. I sent another 100 pages of compromised prose to my agent.

"Not really grabbing me," she said with a sigh. I boxed up the pages, went back to short forms, and finally became comfortable moving between fiction and nonfiction without fear of arrest.

Accept and respect that short forms are fully evolved. They're not baby novels or baby memoirs waiting to grow up.

The Hybrid Genre: Creative Nonfiction

There is a compromise genre for those who straddle the fiction/nonfiction border. Literature was pretty well divided into strict nonfiction or short stories/novels until in 1946, a year after the first atomic bomb was dropped, when John Hersey wrote "Hiroshima."

It was not a novel, but it was as compelling as any piece of fiction. Hersey took a factual event and put a human face on it by telling the true stories of six survivors of the atomic blast. The entire 30,000-word essay was published in *The New Yorker*. "Hiroshima" was followed by Truman Capote's *In Cold Blood*, which also put a human face on a horrific event using the techniques of a fiction writer. The factual dramatization of a murder case brought this emerging genre further into the spotlight.

By the 1970s, Jon Franklin, a newspaper journalist, had also begun to experiment with this hybrid of forms. He began writing news stories with fiction's traditional beginnings, middles, and ends. The result was what we would now call "nonfiction short stories," or "creative nonfiction." Franklin was awarded the first-ever Pulitzer Prize for newspaper feature writing in 1979 and won a second Pulitzer for explanatory journalism in 1985. He says:

> *I was writing fiction at home and nonfiction at work when I finally realized there was no difference in the reader's mind. Both fiction and nonfiction have to touch some reality. Both have to compel, to entertain.*

Franklin explains that although his Pulitzer was a first in that genre, he only helped define the term, and Janet Burroway makes the point that there will always be tension when combining the words "creative" and "nonfiction."

> *The question is, at what point does* creative *embellish itself into* fiction? *On the other hand, at what point does truth squat on the page as inert and unedifying data?*

Again, choosing one genre and then learning to move beyond it or to combine it with another can be a challenge even with such examples to follow. A skill well learned is difficult to unlearn.

I have a student who is a practicing attorney specializing in contract law. He writes legal documents all day long, but he'd like to try a novel, maybe something along the lines of Scott Turow or John Grisham. "What I've noticed," he says about these attempts to write creatively, "is that I write stories using all the elements of fiction, then sum it all up with a closing argument. I write creatively, then wreck it with a speech to the judge" he added (summarizing what he'd just said).

Another student, Tom Woodward, has a Ph.D. and a vast store of analytical writing experience. But when it comes to writing creatively, he has also found that the skills that elevate one genre can hinder another:

> One thing I learned in my 30 years of doing this work is that each step of the logical sequence has to be spelled out. Moreover, it doesn't hurt to say the same thing over again in slightly different language. In creative work, I recognize, this is the impulse to resist. A creative work gains value from ambiguity.

Autobiography Versus Memoir

Identifying exactly where the vestiges of one genre handicap another is half the battle, but actually relinquishing those habits can be a challenge.

A student wrote of being sent away to a strict boarding school in the Austrian Alps at the age of 8. She not only had to adjust to living among strangers, she could not even speak the language of her classmates and teachers. Conditions were harsh and discipline even harsher. She recounted breaking ice in the basin each morning in order to wash her face, along with the other little girls in her dormitory. She wrote of nursing frostbitten toes as a matter of fact: *Recited French lesson, treated frostbite on two toes, had lunch, then free time!* This linear autobiography was of great interest to the writer's family but held the potential to interest a broader audience if she could make it a memoir.

A memoir is more than facts—it reflects upon the events and people who stand out in memory and, in turn, explores their impact. It is not necessarily chronological or complete. How did the little girl who could not speak to anyone, who had to adapt to life in a school without even enough food for its students, become the laughing, accomplished college professor before me? What went on in that little girl's mind and heart? How did she process her pain and shock when, as a seriously ill 8-year-old, she was not allowed to see her own father simply because she had been isolated in a part of the building where the religious order restricted access to visitors?

What you are aware of you can change, but you may find that your natural tendency to stick succinctly to the facts, to make closing arguments, to repeat points, hinders your ability to write well in one genre yet constitutes strengths in another.

Other Genres from Which to Choose

Flash fiction—also known as microfiction, short-short, sudden fiction, and postcard fiction—is a genre where a story can be anywhere from six words to a thousand. By necessity, this form must imply much that it does not say. In its most extreme, a flash fiction story could be: "For sale: wedding band, never worn." Or Joyce Carol Oates's story: "Revenge is living well, without you." Normally, flash fiction is a bit longer and contains all the elements of conventional fiction: a protagonist, a conflict, obstacles, and resolution. But the moment that flash fiction reveals has an afterlife. Flash fiction, done well, is like a tuning fork reverberating after it has been struck. While it resonates, you continue to find the story, the pitch-perfect note.

Nonfiction has its "flash" version as well. Succinctly told essays and bits of memoir are the basis of publications such as Dinty W. Moore's *Brevity*, an online journal of "concise literary nonfiction." These stories of 750 words or less are variably described as "moments not destined to be novels or memoirs." They are magnified moments of experience or "flashes of illumination." Think of short-short nonfiction as a literary lightning strike. You can see everything in a single burst of light—street, car, lamppost—but you only have a second to take in the entire landscape.

Experiment

To experiment with genre, take judgment out of the equation. If you love mysteries, write mysteries. If you love romance novels, write romance novels. Love sci-fi? Write sci-fi. Consider young adult paranormal fiction and romance. You may make a great discovery. Writer and professor Hank Parker says:

> *I never planned to write fiction. The real life stuff was compelling enough: amazing characters, quests and conflicts, struggles and outcomes. And it was my life, my story. But it was one thing to live the story and another to write it. It was hard to capture the essence of people and I was cautious about revealing too much of myself.*
>
> *Then on a dare I participated in National Novel Writing Month. Forget the internal editor, just let it flow; 56,000 words in 25 days. Liberating! I'm now hooked on writing fiction, with its unconstrained, endless possibilities.*

So poke around. Consider writing a children's book. Read Newberry Award–winning books with an eye to craft. Try your hand at writing a play or historical novel or travel essay. And poetry is not only a genre but a training ground for writing well in any form.

Learning to write poetry teaches you the power of metaphor and economy of language. Poetry is a way writers learn to see.

Exchange "genre" for "genuine." Write what you love without thought as to the popularity of the form because if you are engaged, others will be engaged, and that's a fundamental necessity for publishing anything.

I flew out to Utah to visit a friend in Park City a while back. It's a tiny mining town in the Wasatch Range that transformed itself into a posh ski resort when the vein of silver ran out. I was in a place of transition and trying on a change of scene. Maybe, like Park City itself, I could find a new identity. Maybe my writing would reflect a new identity as well.

Three days later, I was on a plane headed east. The airline had been stripped of all amenities in recent years, such as, well, food. The company distracts passengers from this fact through the upbeat personalities of its crew members, most of whom could be standup comedians. A flight attendant dressed like she was going to a picnic was demonstrating the plane's safety features.

"If we unexpectedly lose cabin pressure," she explained, "the oxygen masks will deploy. If you are traveling with more than one child, put on your mask first before assisting them." She grinned. "Then pick the child with the most potential."

Everything you write should be loved and nurtured. Every genre in which you create work is as much a part of you as a son or daughter. But for sheer joy and its attendant success, concentrate your energy on the child of your heart, whether or not that child is the most popular of your offspring.

21
Writing Classes and a Wider Audience

> *"A creative writing class may be one of the last places you can go where your life still matters."*
> —Richard Hugo, "In Defense of the Writing Class"

It began like the opening of a novel; a short plane ride, a breezy ferry trip, flirting, photography, and a wide-eyed drive around Martha's Vineyard. The October morning was cool as I parked in a meadow near a one-room cottage. Inside, twelve people sat in a circle—a candle and crystals in the middle. Hmmm. A long, thin woman with a huge smile and welcoming eyes sat cross-legged near the wall. "This week we'll write stories from the heart, read them aloud, and tell each other what we love about them." No criticism, no suggestions. Well, I thought, that's all right. I'll enjoy The Vineyard, write a little, and feel really good about myself. My writing won't improve much. Wrong.

I learned I can write from the heart for fifteen minutes, hear good things about that effort, and be changed as a writer forever. I began to find my voice. They called me "a weaver," they called me that over and over again. And now, I weave when I write, and I feel good about doing it.

—Margaret Foster

Even as the number of writing workshops and programs has soared
in the last two decades, there is debate over whether creative writing
can be taught. A professor at Oxford University asked me about this
as we were walking across the campus one evening. Full disclosure:
it was a dusky English autumn and I was on a ghost tour. Apparently,
some pretty spooky things appear in the windows of ancient ivy-
covered buildings at Oxford and materialize suddenly in bell towers.
The professor was both esteemed in her field (history) and a student
of unexplained phenomena. She asked me whether creative writing
can be taught in a way that was clearly a statement to the contrary.
"You teach *creative writing? Can* that be taught?" I swear, if you say
this with a British accent it is not a question.

Obviously writing can be taught. You can learn a great deal on
your own, but when you are ready, taking a workshop can accelerate
the process. It can require a good bit of courage because in most
creative writing classes participants' work is "critiqued," a word that
sounds a lot like "criticized." A small group of strangers reads and
comments on your story while you remain silent. It is important
that you not participate in the discussion so you won't become distracted by the impulse to defend your work. After all, the theory
goes, you can't follow your published work around explaining it.
Unfortunately, this often feels as if you have been gagged and tied
up while strangers run off with your baby.

When They Are Good

A workshop can be an invaluable experience. Your story is carefully
read by intelligent people who appreciate and nurture your afore-
mentioned baby. They improve your baby's attempts at communication. They make insightful suggestions that you can see immediately
will improve your offspring's chance of survival.

In a good workshop, the leader stays in control of the discussion, guiding it to remain productive. If no one sees the finer points of your story, the instructor will point them out while protecting you from well-meaning people who want to point at you while they speak.

In a great workshop, you leave validated with new ideas for revision. Careful readers will have shown you that your lead paragraph is slow but your piece ignites in the second paragraph and is ablaze by the third. Careful readers will note that your title is working against the understanding of the piece, that you can cut the whole last page and lose nothing. This kind of feedback makes you grateful you live in a democracy—groups are smart. It's the difference between work that sizzles and the slush pile. It's exhilarating.

Where to Find Instruction

Start with a writing class at the nearest community college or university. Go to one of the summer workshops held around the country. Often these are held on college campuses or in a beautiful location, like California's Napa Valley. You can find writing workshops in virtually any state. You can write in an Irish castle or overlooking a Venetian canal as well.

Google "writing instruction" to investigate programs or take an entire class online. Join book groups that discuss the ways in which books are structured and the use of craft. Look into graduate writing programs. Consider a low-residency program that allows you to continue working and living at home with limited time on campus. Not only will these options mentor your craft, you will make connections, developing relationships with other writers, authors, publishers, and agents.

Learn to decode biographical information when you choose an instructor so that you will be making informed choices. Widely published? Where? Print or online? Self-published or in local, regional, or national publications? Nominated for or won? Award-winning? What award? Attended or graduated? Does numerous actually mean two? Check out the instructor's website. Read some of his work. A workshop leader who is currently writing and submitting work is dealing with the same challenges you are. The shared experience can create a vibrant and intimate dynamic in the room.

How to Be a Good Workshop Member

One of the first workshops I attended included a very attractive and fragile woman who had a look of perpetual alarm, even when it was not her story being critiqued. The whites of her eyes showed all the way around the luminous dark irises as if she had just heard the shatter of glass at the back door on a stormy night.

Her memoir was about her three sons; stories about the boys playing together, competing for her affection, being protective of their mom. Jake, Adam, and Gregory were dark-haired youngsters, very close in age, with distinctive personalities. By the time they were sleeping in the same bed and eating out of the same bowl, it became clear the boys were Labradoodles.

The gentle compassion with which this woman's work was handled by the workshop instructor, a much more advanced soul than I, was the real lesson. A good leader will lift everyone up. Everyone who makes a sincere effort is entitled to your respect as a human being and everyone's work can improve, but more than that, you cannot know the pain and loss that may have prompted another writer's story. Assume that if you did know, you would be in awe of her courage to simply show up in her life every day. Sometimes what another student has to teach you is not found on the page, like compassion, like empathy.

A writing workshop can jump-start an entire career or reinvigorate one that is flagging. It can also demoralize, destroy confidence, and confuse.

And When They Are Bad ...

My colleague Ann was at a plateau in her work and attended a workshop being run by a famous writer. It was expensive when you included hotel and airfare, but the benefits sounded promising. Ann invited a writer friend to share the adventure and to ease the social awkwardness of being thrust into a fairly intimate environment with strangers.

For three days Ann and her friend met for meditation warm-ups and workshops with the famous writer. They analyzed each other's work. "What did the writer mean by 'heart like a blown fuse'?" the group mused. They practiced their craft en masse: *Two minutes or less! Write about life as a kumquat!* Which reminded Ann of why she had changed her major from drama to English in college. The memories still haunted her: *Be bacon, frying!* On the plane home, Ann's friend was 40 pages into a newly inspired memoir and Ann was staring out the window, depressed and paralyzed.

Workshops can fail to be rewarding experiences for many reasons. Sometimes your classmates are overworked and didn't read the piece until they came to class, and one or two may have anger issues. The workshop leader isn't really in control of the group dynamic and doesn't redirect or keep people from addressing you directly— people to whom, by the rules of engagement, you may not respond. No one bothers to point out what is working in your story because they assume you already know all the good stuff and just get right down to pointing out all the places the story fails. Sometimes people approach this as a moral obligation.

All writers need to hear the good stuff. They need to hear it first and they need to hear it last. Writers are not going to become arrogant, conceited, or lazy when work is praised. They are going to become confident, which makes them willing to take risks. They are going to learn to trust their intuition, to write even more, which is the only way anyone ever improves.

In the worst-case scenario, which I have witnessed, the workshop leader isn't adequately prepared. A good piece that needs very little shaping is belabored in lieu of a class plan. Unable to make any substantial improvements, students wanting to please by making an effort begin to suggest wilder and wilder ideas. "Have you thought about rewriting the entire story from another tense and changing the gender of the protagonist?" These are most likely sensationally bad ideas.

Over the years I've noticed bad ideas are often couched in the phrase, "I wanted to know more about ____." Sometimes this is a legitimate response, but often it is a euphemism for "I wanted to know more about this character *not* in your story, because I am so totally uninterested in the story itself." If you hear this a lot, read between the lines. Rather than graft a new limb onto a failing tree, try looking at the trunk and strengthening its base.

It is possible that you may hear well-articulated thoughts from people who didn't read carefully. Don't get swayed by a polished delivery of bad advice. Understand that group dynamics nearly always contain a contrary. If the whole group likes your piece, someone will have to differ. It is human nature. (And I know at least one of you is thinking, "No, it's not.")

Making Workshop Exercises Productive

As Ann and her friend discovered, writing instructors sometimes design timed exercises to give you a direction and a sense of urgency that will allow you to power over your natural inhibitions. You may be told, for instance, to write everything you know about those kumquats.

Your mind goes blank. You can't remember exactly what a kumquat is. Vegetable? Fruit? Have you ever actually tasted one?

Your neighbor is vigorously scribbling. Across the table, someone is flipping his paper over to write on the reverse side, having filled up the front. You have options:

1. Write about the fear, the paralysis, the fact that you've been brought to your knees, laid low by a kumquat.

2. Or try: "I don't know a thing about kumquats, but I do know my rhubarb," and write about rhubarb or whatever else catches your attention.

3. Or try speaking to the kumquat: address it, tell it of your dilemma, ask its advice.

4. Or let the kumquat speak. Maybe it has a story of its own to tell.

Just don't interpret an inability to jump into every exercise as a significant reflection of your talent. If you feel you are too vulnerable for this process, continue to mentor yourself with books on craft or find an individual writing instructor.

Teaching Your Instructor

As a writing student, you are going to teach your instructor invaluable things if she lets you. You will teach her to be prepared, that teaching is like mindfulness training: she simply must be present no matter what distractions are at hand.

You will demonstrate that learning is about relationships and that you and your classmates need and want to know each other. The fact is that you will learn from your classmates as much as you will learn from your instructor, if you are given the opportunity. Initiate discussion; talk to each other, even if you must do so on the break.

As a unit, you are going to demonstrate that no matter how carefully your instructor reads, she will not catch everything; that groups are wise; that she will teach best what she most needs to remember. Find a teacher who will cheer you on, nurturing your tenacity and creative spirit. Find a teacher who is, in spirit, also a student. Allow yourself to trust in her belief in you.

Writing classes may or may not improve your work. There are so many variables—from the quality of the instruction to the effort and talent of the participants. But a writing workshop is an opportunity to see your work in the greater context of the world before it is published—to see if and how it affects people. It is an opportunity to learn discernment and empathy—to find and celebrate siblings in the writing life.

Trey Miller, a former student, said:

> For years I considered myself a "non-practicing writer." I enjoyed writing, and was competent at it, but I never made the time to do it with any focus or discipline. Attending a writing workshop gave me a better understanding of the mechanics and provided practical tools.

Miller also suggested some practical tools for those who critique—a set of rubber stamps that might save time and labor. He sent photos of the stamps via the Internet. They are available as a set with the following sentiments: "I liked it better last week," "Keep searching," "I'm not convinced," "Let me know when you finish," and my absolute favorite: "Are *you* happy with this?"

Because in the end, that's all that really matters.

Part 4

Continuing the Journey into the World

22

Forming a Writing Support Group

"Feedback is the breakfast of champions."
—Ken Blanchard and Spencer Johnson, *The One Minute Manager*

*I think, to a poet, the human community is like the community of
birds to a bird, singing to each other. Love is one of the reasons we
are singing to one another, love of language itself, love of sound, love
of singing itself, and love of the other birds.*

—Sharon Olds

Writers have long been stereotyped as loners and quirky miscreants
whose bridge to the world is the written word because their actual
participation in it is so dysfunctional. Think suffering. Think garret.
Think shuffling around in your slippers with a glass of bourbon and
a cigarette.

In reality, writers are incredibly normal, happy people who have
partners and children, change the batteries in their smoke alarms,
and adopt rescue dogs. Remember where we began? Writers write
because they love the world. Although writing takes place in isolation most of the time, writers still need to socialize, to connect. Like
birds that sing alone on a branch, they also gather in flocks to fly.

Creating a Group

Sometimes the chemistry of a workshop is so exceptional that some class members decide to continue meeting on their own, which can be a lot like trying to go back to the place where you spent your honeymoon. The dynamic is totally different as familiarity builds. It also takes some time for the group to find its equilibrium without a leader. Still, there are writing groups that began as a class of strangers that continue to meet for years because the members came to trust and value one another's opinions. They become a family—which is another group you didn't design but enjoy and trust. Writing classes can be costly, while a writing group is free, and the long-term commitment is a far different experience than a 10-week class. "Like branding steers or embalming the dead, teaching was a profession I had never seriously considered," said David Sedaris in "The Learning Curve." Maybe, like Sedaris, you never considered being a teacher either. Well, in a group without a leader, you are one.

Set up your rules clearly: How many pages may each person turn in? How often will you meet? Where? How long will each meeting be? Will food be served? Who supplies it? How will work be distributed? How much in advance of each meeting? How are new members recruited?

Discussing Another Writer's Work

Good feedback, given in the right way, can make an enormous difference in people's ability to grow. Good feedback always empowers people. It points them in the direction of their next step and makes it easier for them to take it. All teaching is learning. All empowerment of others is self-empowerment.

Author and teacher Sanaya Roman knows that although we can fear sharing work, sometimes the greater challenge is being able to comment intelligently on someone else's work, especially without a moderator. You hold such power. It is so easy to be clumsy with it.

If the story being discussed is particularly engaging, it's not so difficult to jump in without a referee. But if the story needs a lot of work, the group sits around the hostess's coffee table as if each is holding a grenade and no one wants to pull the pin.

Sometimes members simply make general comments. "I've always loved stories about food," someone ventures, taking a big bite of brownie and nodding encouragingly to someone else. Or they hold back until one brave soul says something more critical than intended, and suddenly it's a pile-on. You'd think that people who are about to have their own work discussed would be careful, but I've been guilty of gargantuan insensitivity myself. Sometimes you are so sure you are right or so excited about this great piece of advice you're about to give that you get carried away and speak with an authority that isn't warranted.

Passion isn't permission, nor is it an indicator that you are right. Print that out and tape that to your folder or forehead.

I remember discussing the novel of a lovely woman who had entrusted me with this honor when we had agreed to swap work. It was polished and well-written, the setting was fine, the characters real, their dialogue believable. They had a problem to solve; they had subplots as well. It felt as professionally written as any book I'd ever picked up at Barnes and Noble.

I couldn't think of a way to improve it because it could be exchanged with so many published books just like it. That's when it struck me that what was right with the book was what was wrong with it. It was generic, ordinary. As well written as it was, it was a story you've read a thousand times.

So with great excitement I started telling my writer-acquaintance-victim that her book was unoriginal. It needed more of *her* in it, needed to be about her very specific character's lost love, which had been lost in an unpredictable way and now hung in jeopardy.

We were seated side by side on the couch and once I got going, I became more and more articulate, reiterating my discovery in ever more expressive ways. Finally I turned to look at the author to see if she was as excited about my incredible insights as I was and saw her face was so red she'd clearly been holding her breath since I'd begun my analysis. Her eyes glittered not with excitement but *tears*.

I don't know why it hadn't occurred to me that hearing her book was bland, predictable, and boring would be difficult. I still haven't forgiven myself. But it certainly is easy to understand why group members fear commenting on one another's work, so here are some things to remember.

The story is not yours to change, so don't change it. If you feel a change is necessary, however, see if you can suggest one or two ideas worth exploring rather than expressing vague dissatisfaction.

Start with the big picture, the macrocosm. What general observations can you make about the story? Were you drawn into the plot? By what? At what point? What about the theme resonated with you? What universality did you relate to? Were you surprised? Delighted? Charmed? Educated? Entertained? Moved? Stunned? Were you affected by the story?

Ask questions about the piece. Questions to be asked and discussed, not asked and answered.

We've already said we need to start with the good stuff, but what if you don't see anything and don't have an instructor to find it for you? Look more closely. Can you applaud the writer's originality? The energy of the piece? The honesty of it? The writer's stretch, even if it exceeded her grasp? Support the other writer's vulnerability by selecting and highlighting her success. Then say how you feel about the story; then say what the story *may* need to succeed from your perspective. You are not right. You do not have *the* truth, you just have a perspective, *your* truth.

I was 18 the first time I was in a writing group. A soulful boy who hung around my dorm a lot playing his guitar had turned in a poem. I had a crush on this boy, mainly because he played his guitar like Cat Stevens, who had not yet become Yusuf Islam.

The poem gave me my first insight into this boy's personal history. He wrote of walking back from class one evening and seeing colors reflected in a rain puddle. The reflected world was broken, rearranged. It was the most beautiful poem I'd ever heard— a metaphor for divorce and its aftermath, the pain of loss, the murky waters.

I was first to share, undeniably pleased that I had instinctively known what the poem was about, that the poet and I obviously had a similar sensibility. Maybe we'd walk back to the dorm together after the group ended for the evening. I was pretty choked up, too, having divorced parents myself, and after what I hoped was an astute analysis but was probably a pretty gushy minute or two, I stopped speaking so he could respond. He was quiet for a moment, but then that was his way. His cool way. I held my breath.

"It was about a dead bird," he whispered without looking up.

The best thing about the lessons learned in a writing group, a workshop, or a class is this: they become a cautionary tale that stays with you. They become the voice in your head, the warning system that says make no assumptions, be alert and be kind, and don't forget to highlight the good stuff. What you take from a group will become the best editor you've ever had, and the memories (trust me) will stay with you the rest of your life.

23

Publishing and Rejection

"If your ship doesn't come in, swim out to meet it."
—Jonathan Winters

*To keep writing, learning, and persevering despite rejections is
a supremely assertive act. It defies reason, it scoffs at logic, but
the antidote to the aches and pain of rejection is that single line
all writers long to read: [New York Publisher] agrees to publish
[I Reject Rejection!] by I. M. Author.*

—Mark Bailey

Writing is an art, but publishing is a business, a competitive, difficult business that can lead one to seek out consultants. About every five years I visit Connie Janey. Connie lives in a clapboard farmhouse about 15 miles out of town on a gentle swell of cornfields she calls "Tarot Rise." Jeans and a sweatshirt, no makeup except a welcoming smile, Connie tells fortunes by reading tarot cards at her kitchen table, which makes her a bit of a life coach with props. "What can you tell me about my writing?" I always ask. "Your writing …" she repeats, squinting at the cards. Connie chain smokes throughout the entire reading, which clearly means she *can* see the future, and hers isn't death from lung cancer.

I come because the news about publishing is so dire. I want encouragement. I want help with the grim numbers. You've read them.

Thirty to fifty *thousand* submissions a year sent to top literary reviews. That's thousands of submissions sent to *quarterlies*. Agents so overworked they can only read new manuscripts after hours and on weekends, agents who routinely get 20 new submissions a day.

A Change in Attitude, a Change in Fortune

Being inundated with the new realities of the publishing industry makes "I'll never be published" feel like a fact. And you suffer as if this glum prediction *is* a fact. But the truth, as we established earlier, is that you selectively produce, seek, notice, and draw to you evidence that what you *believe* is true whether or not it is. A slight digression to make this point:

If you have any doubt that your attitude affects your publishing success, bear in mind the placebo response is the most extensively documented and indisputable example that we experience as true what we believe is true. We've become inured to how actually awesome this fact is because we equate "placebo" with "gullible." That's not how the major pharmaceutical companies see it. What it means to them is that *half* of all new drugs that fail in late stage trials fail because of their inability to beat *the power of thought*. Big Pharma has lost so many new drugs to this phenomenon that they are considering ways to harness it instead of competing with it. So should you.

It is hard to accept that without conscious intervention our brains essentially sabotage our writing efforts, but it is a survival mechanism at work. We are biologically hardwired to pay more attention to unpleasant feelings than to pleasant ones. Optimistic Neanderthals didn't peer into the underbrush looking for lions before they plopped down to make fire or gnaw on something. Consequently … those optimists were not your ancestors. The anxiety-prone pessimists hiding in the nearest cave were your ancestors, and the legacy continues.

Studies show that if you hear something both positive and negative about a stranger, you'll take the negative view because it's safer. Sure, he could be nice, but he could also be a serial killer. Likewise, you'll spot an angry face in a crowd of happy people faster than you will spot one happy face in an angry crowd. Again, it's safer. We evolved in ways that ensure our survival, and the same is true of your writing. Expecting to fail is a way in which you protect yourself from disappointment. By shielding yourself from disappointment, your writing survives as you keep plugging away.

But a change in perspective can change everything. You don't need a hundred publishers any more than you need a hundred buyers for your house. You need one. Words create thoughts which create feelings which are a form of energy which is a form of influence. Think acceptance, you attract acceptance. This ability is a tool, like a hammer. You can build a house with it only when you stop hitting yourself in the head with it. "Argue for your limitations and sure enough, they're yours," writes author Richard Bach.

So change the story you are telling yourself about publishing to a positive one and, as we learned about intuition, your contacts, relationships, choices about subjects, and where to submit work will shift to support your new reality. You'll find creative ideas about new markets coming to mind, people who could help you, publications you've overlooked. You will always draw to you what you most profoundly believe and imagine most vividly.

Creative Ways to Publish

An increasingly popular way to get your work out there is to forgo print publishers by using the Internet. That means submitting to online publications, or to the online versions of print publications. Getting your foot in the door in the online version can help you move into the print version at some point in the future if your work is well received. Another way to publish online can be by writing a blog. You can start one, of course, or you can look into writing for one that is already established, like Beliefnet or The Huffington Post.

Perhaps you are not a household name, but you have an idea for an interesting subject. Consider compiling an anthology of other people's work on your topic, adding a story of your own, and editing the collection. A friend collected letters between mothers and daughters that were published and promoted in the month before Mother's Day. Another friend is interviewing older people and creating an anthology of their most moving stories. One enterprising writing coach asked best-selling authors to share their favorite writing exercises and published a book of them. Contact famous people for their stories to give your book more commercial salability. People like to talk about themselves. You might be surprised at who is willing to contribute.

Consider taking matters into your own hands. There was a time when people hid the fact that they were considering self-publishing the way they might have hidden the fact that they were considering a tattoo. There was a time when self-publishing was the equivalent of wearing knock-off Prada or a fake Rolex. But the industry is not what it used to be. The term "vanity press" is falling by the wayside as more good authors choose this option. Numerous sites on the Internet offer packages that allow you to customize the degree of help you need and therefore control costs.

In addition, some major publishers now have a self-publishing arm. For a reasonable fee, you can publish your book through their self-publishing imprint and receive virtually all the benefits of a conventional publishing contract. You may be required to do your own promotion, but that has also become the case with many established publishers. Because self-publishing is gaining momentum every day, you can also find methods for distributing your book and having it reviewed in reputable places, which will help you sell it.

Another option is entering contests that guarantee publication as part of the prize.

But what if what you long for is your name as *author* (not publisher, editor, or contest winner) on a short story, essay, or book of your own work—a real book made of, at the very least, trade paperback-quality paper with an illustration on the cover?

The desire to publish sits like the nightmare in your closet. You can contain it, but you know it is there, panting and thumping around. You can pretend not to think about it, in which case you are probably deep in denial. You can also pretend you don't care and just take classes for the rest of your life. But you have more influence and options than you probably imagine. First, you should know what publication will and won't do for you.

Acceptance: A Natural High

The first time you sell a story, the news feels like a caffeine overdose. Your pulse races, your surroundings become surreal, and you punch in phone numbers to call your spouse and two best friends as if you have won the state lottery. You are speeding, euphoric; if you get pulled over behind the wheel of a car in the next hour, you'll fail the field sobriety test.

By the time the piece is published, you'll be more anxious than high. Will they have spelled your name right? Yes. Changed things without telling you? Yes. Inexplicably cut the best parts? Yes. The point being that the euphoria of publishing lasts a very short time; in fact, it's often over before the fact. Moreover, it can be a long time between highs.

The Business and the Art

Besides the quick fix, what else does publication do for you? If the
story comes out as you wrote it and it is something you love, publication allows you to share yourself, to give a gift to others. It allows
you to leave something behind that lives on after you are gone.

If you are published by a company you respect, you also gain
credibility. You are recognized by others. You are building a resumé.
You can give readings, apply for jobs and grants. You can say, "I am
a writer" without feeling like someone is going to tap you on the
shoulder with a grim, "Says who?"

But I have also come to class to find a book left on my desk anony-
mously, like a baby on the church steps. Glancing around the room, I'll
see one student making intense eye contact: *Please pick it up—it's mine
but I can't claim it.* These are the students who put the business before
the art and published work about which they are now sheepish; work
they know is not their best, or that has been published in places for
which they feel they should apologize. And although pseudonyms can
be a good idea for any number of reasons, I don't think I've ever had a
friend say, "I wrote this under a pseudonym and it's great!"

Better to write what you love and *then* seek a home for it than
to try to come up with a clever idea to get published. That way if it
takes a long time, or never happens at all, you spent the days, weeks,
and years of your life doing something gratifying and producing
something of which you can be proud.

*There's so much advice about submitting your work to a publisher.
"Shop it." "Research it." "Don't be greedy." Okay, I've only been
published two times in very small publications, but I say, "Enjoy
it." I like the kind of advice that tells you to "form your stories
with love and hard work and then send them out the same way you
send your children out the door—when they're 'ready enough.'"*

—Margaret Foster

When You Are Ready to Submit

Read the publications to which you'd like to submit work. Become so familiar with their subjects, voice, and style that you can shape your work accordingly while being true to your own voice. Read writers' guidelines *after* you have finished the piece, after you have written authentically, and see if you need to tweak it a bit or whether your work is too far from their style and you should search for a publisher that is a better fit.

Magazines and literary reviews have editorial voices. Don't expect any of them to publish you because your story is so refreshingly different from their norm. Finding the right publisher for your work is like buying shoes. You can try on a hundred pairs in many styles until you find a comfortable pair of quality shoes that looks great. But don't try to change the size of your feet.

Research markets online. There are many excellent free sites; research by subject, by category, by region. Explore books like *The Literary Marketplace*, *Writer's Market*, and *The International Directory of Little Magazines and Small Presses*.

Follow your intuition. If you sense your work is right for a publication, keep on sending it. Develop a relationship with the editor by responding to his suggestions. As Mark Bailey said, persevere. And as John Gardner said: "The qualities that make a true artist are nearly the same qualities that make a true athlete."

When you are ready to submit, always include a cover letter of no more than one page with your manuscript whether you are submitting electronically or through the mail. (Always check the preferred method for each publication.) The tone of your letter should be professional, succinct, and engaging. The cover letter is essentially a calling card; it accompanies single stories or articles and simply states your contact information, what you have enclosed, and why it has been sent to that editor in particular. It also succinctly references your credentials.

A query letter, in contrast, is a pitch—a sales tool—asking that the editor give you permission to send him or her your completed manuscript, book, article proposal, or anything of substantial length that would require a commitment of time for the editor to read. A query letter will open with a fascinating fact or engaging anecdote about your subject to pique the editor's interest. It will focus on the content of the proposed manuscript and its potential readership. Its sole purpose is to secure an invitation to send your work, which will keep it out of the slush pile.

Whether you are writing a simple cover letter or a query, do not try to be funny: too subjective and way too risky. Don't be too familiar. You think "casual," the editor thinks "presumptuous."

List your credentials professionally. Do not address editors by their first names. Do not address the editor by his job title, as in "Dear Editor." Don't try to summarize your entire story. If your cover letter gives you any credibility at all, the editor is going to at least flip over to your opening page. If you have written well enough, he'll keep reading. If not, the best cover letter in the world won't sell your story. *Do* let him know you respect his publication; that it is your first choice as a market. Always enclose a self-addressed stamped envelope for a reply and send it off hoping never to see it again.

Good news never arrives in your own envelope.

Before you go to the post office to mail your submission, perform your personal good luck ritual. I know you have one.

Keep a record of where you submitted each piece, the date sent, and the number of weeks before you can fairly expect a reply.

Submit work simultaneously. You will not actually be arrested or have your tires slashed. You must immediately notify all editors to whom you have submitted, however, if your piece is accepted.

Lastly, never insult an editor. Editors of national magazines say it is not unheard of to receive submissions accompanied by a dressing down along the lines of "You probably won't have the intelligence or insight to recognize how great this book is, and you'll probably be no brighter than the last seven editors who lost out on the opportunity to publish it, but I'm going to give you a chance. Enclosed is my manuscript, *All About Me: The Early Years*. You may call me tonight before eight o'clock with your answer."

Rejection

My mother, who was an aspiring writer as a young woman, once received the following rejection letter:

> *Dear Contributor,*
> *Thank you for sending us the six pieces of paper. Unfortunately, somebody wrote all over them.*

The rejection was from my father—a witty if not empathetic man.

There are a lot of rejections on the way to an acceptance, which is tough because rejection can make you question your worth as a human being. This may seem extreme, but it is not an unusual reaction. Rejection really is, of course, simply someone's opinion that your work is not right for their publication at this time. Whew. Like choosing a partner, you are going to have to date a lot before you find what you're looking for. Then the chemistry has to be mutual. Again, the message is to persevere.

Personal rejection letters, where the editor has scrawled, "Sorry about this one, send more," are almost as good as an acceptance. Then there are the rejections that come with a return envelope in which you are asked to send a financial contribution to the review. You probably won't do this.

The worst rejections are the form letters, which nowadays are not letters at all but tiny preprinted notes the size of an index card or smaller. Sometimes they come attached to the title page of your manuscript, which has been ripped from the text. It's sort of like a kidnapper has sent proof that he has disposed of your loved one.

The worst rejection I ever received was from *The Iowa Review* in the fall of 2000. My submission was a short story. The rejection was a poem. A small, mean poem. It came on a tiny piece of paper attached to my cover letter, where I had shared the relevant, professional facts about myself by way of introduction. That made it even meaner. Untitled and unsigned yet formally preprinted on *Iowa Review* stationery, the poem went like this:

> This is just to say
> We have taken some plums
> We found in our mail box.
> You were hoping they would be
> Yours. Forgive us
> Others seemed
> Sweeter
> Or colder
> More bold
> Or whatever.

That was it. It seemed smug and cowardly and personal, and it hurt exceptionally.

Not everyone takes rejection letters lying down, however, and the impulse to try to explain why the editor is wrong, or to negotiate a second chance, is always there. When the rejection is particularly disappointing, it's tempting to send the editor a rejection of your own.

Dear Sir:

Thank you for sending me the enclosed rejection letter. While I read your letter with interest, it does not meet my editorial needs at this time. My rejection of your rejection does not necessarily reflect upon its quality. I get so many I must sometimes return perfectly good rejections. I cannot comment in detail, but it might help you to know that your prose didn't knock my socks off and your adjectives were, I'm sorry, a little tired. I'm looking for fresher, more original rejections. I'm returning your rejection to you confident that you will find a home for it elsewhere.

What Publication Will Not Do

Publication will not make you better looking, the caveat to that being the fact that everyone looks better when they smile. You can smile anyway.

It is not a sustainable high and it will not make you more popular, unless you have published a best-selling novel or been reviewed in *The New York Times*, in which case you will attract name droppers who like to say they are friends with celebrities.

Publication does not fix your relationships; it does not mean you will be happy or that you will even be published again. If your first book does not sell well, even if it is well received by critics, you will find it is far more difficult to publish a second book than the first. You are only as good, they say, as your last book. In the words of Alfred Kazin:

In every real sense, the writer writes in order to teach himself, to understand himself, to satisfy himself; the publishing of his ideas is a curious anticlimax.

We all want to be published. We want our work to be shared, but publication is a whistle stop on the journey. It is not your destination. Publication is only a place you get to pause while the engine idles; wave to bystanders, then move on.

24

Attending a Writers' Conference

"There are two ways of spreading light; to be the candle or the mirror that reflects it."
—Eudora Welty

I'll look into the writers' conference, but I would most likely not enjoy attending (even as I recognize it'd be good for me). I don't like travel, or large groups of people. I don't particularly enjoy talking about writing. I'd much rather quietly tend to the chickens, work in the garden, or mindlessly play basketball with people who've probably never read a book cover to cover in their lives.

—Seth Clabough

Whereas dermatologists and coin collectors look forward to their shindigs, writers wince and delay registration until a friend registers for them, or they miss the deadline. We're not unfriendly; we're just ambivalent. We've become accustomed to what at first was a necessary isolation. Sort of like when you were sent to your room for an hour as a kid because you had lied about feeding the cat, but when your mother finally said you could come out, you said you loved it in there and actually wanted to stay longer. In fact, it was so great in there you might just not come out until dinner, or the next solar eclipse.

Familiarity doesn't mean something is good for you.

Author Barbara Klein Moss speaks of the richness of the offerings versus the relentless intensity of the experience as a fellow at The Bread Loaf Writers' Conference.

A day at a conference can seem like a week of ordinary life; a week there like a month anywhere else. It really is like living in a parallel universe: a village of writers where everyone shares the same passions as you do. In that sense, a conference is a good corrective to the larger world that many writers inhabit, where their choice of profession may be regarded as incomprehensible or downright subversive. But the single focus and sheer abundance of riches can be wearing over time. After a week of fine lectures and readings, workshops, conversations, I felt that I couldn't take in one more artful sentence. I wanted to make pasta, read a newspaper, flee back to the solitude of my desk.

The paradox is that as reluctant as writers are to mingle with large groups of their kind, writing conferences are proliferating right along with the surge in writing programs nationwide. So why do so many writers eventually, with high hopes and deep suspicions, attend?

Tote Bags and Other Takeaways

Writers' conferences take place all over the country all year long. Sometimes they are a day or weekend, but they can be a week or two. They typically are held on a college campus, or at a conference retreat or a hotel. At the three- and four-day conferences, you can expect to find display tables and booths set up by publishers promoting their houses, magazines, and literary reviews. There will be representatives from MFA programs located all over the country as well. Panels will be offered composed of authors, agents, editors, publishers, literary rock stars, experts, academics, and university writing program directors. There will be author signings every five minutes. The one-week and two-week residential gatherings focus more on workshops, lectures, readings, and developing relationships with other writers.

If you register ahead of time, you may get a discount on the fee, and you will have time to select which of the seminars you wish to attend. Expect it to be difficult to choose because invariably the two or three you are interested in will be given at the same time. Seminar topics will range from discussion of craft to philosophical questions to copyright law. There will be readings throughout the conference, hosted by various literary reviews. A keynote address, most often given by the biggest award-winning author the conference can secure, will be a big draw. Be sure to check out that one.

You will discover publications to which you can submit work and get to shake hands with the editorial staff. You can pick up free copies as well. You can meet in person the editor who has previously accepted your work—or rejected it. These people will surprise you—by how friendly and welcoming they are and, in many cases, by how young. You can learn something new at the seminars and ask questions of authors you've admired for years.

Many conferences also allow you to meet with literary agents for brief appointments to discuss your work and get some free feedback. You can also pitch your work directly to publishers. This is not to be compared to a mass audition for reality television. I do know people who have secured publishers for their novels this way.

There are often informal cocktail parties and sometimes dances at which you have further opportunities to meet and mingle. Just be sure that the social aspects are not the substance of what is being offered. Mary Ann Treger says:

> *Maybe I expected too much from my writers conference. I'd only been freelancing a few years and wanted to pick the brains of the pros but the social aspects of the conference took priority. One*

*seminar, "How to Write for Social Media," was cut to an hour
because the bus was ready to leave for free city tours! While it was
fun to network with other freelancers, and hey, who doesn't love a
good party, the conference wasn't what I expected.*

The Reluctance

With all these benefits to attending a writers' conference, you might
be asking yourself, "So what *is* the downside?" Why do I actually
feel suspicious or as if I need to protect myself from this experience
in some way?

Your reluctance is longing. You can gussy it up to look like fru-
gality (yes, there is a fee) or commitment to your work (yes, you will
not be writing for a day or so) or as "none of the topics interest me"
(*seriously?*), but it is still yearning that makes us chew on the pen
before signing the check or initiating PayPal.

The vision of moving through crowds of other writers with their
almost palpable longing calls up our own. Seeing, firsthand, all the
other writers out there who are passionate, interesting, brilliant,
dedicated, and, in fact, not even a little bit weird, is scary. Attendance puts faces and personalities on abstractions like "we publish
only about 1 percent of the manuscripts we receive." Suddenly you
are looking your competition in the eye. Hearing about others'
successes is depressing. Even seeing the number of publishing
opportunities that are out there cranks up the longing and the
anxiety. How are you going to find the time to write and submit
work to all these new places you've just learned about?

At a conference, you come face to face with reality. Writers pack
the same seminars in which you are interested. Sometimes you can't
even squeeze in the room. All those avid, ambitious writers wanting
what you want when you know there's not enough to go around.
And then you board the crazy train.

You've been writing a novel based on an obscure religious sect founded in twelfth-century Japan. Your fear is that if you put yourself in the proximity of so many inquiring minds, all searching for original ideas for *their* novels, one may actually be able to perform a Mr. Spock mind-meld and lift "fascinating twelfth-century religious sect" right out of your brain. Or, you are going to discover that whatever made you think of this heretofore unique idea made three people from the Midwest and one from Florida think of it, too. You just don't want to know.

Best- and Worst-Case Scenarios

Do the work of researching your conference ahead of time. Check out the panelists, study the opportunities, shop around, and ask other writers who have attended about their experiences. Check airfare prices; hotels usually have a discount you can get in on if you register in advance.

Wear comfortable clothes, particularly comfortable shoes. You will probably receive some kind of tote bag, but bring one for all the reviews, journals, business cards, pamphlets, publishers' catalogues, and freebies you'll pick up.

Work out in your head the quickest route between seminars because, just as in junior high when you had 15 minutes to eat lunch, now you'll have 15 minutes between workshops that can be spread out in separate venues *and* to eat lunch. Wear a watch.

The worst-case scenarios are the oversold rooms, where people have taken every seat, are lining the walls and holding the door open in order for people sitting in the hallway to be able to hear, which they won't. The worst-case scenario has people clogging the popular panels by sitting on the floor with their legs stuck out, the coughers, the talkers, and those panelists who may be smart but are not good performers. They stand up and read academic papers in a monotone. Don't be shy about walking out at the first opportunity where your retreat won't create a disturbance. You paid money for this, and staying put just to be polite makes as much sense as not repainting a room when you know you've picked the wrong color.

As Jane Elkin writes:

> *Going to a writers' conference is a bit like going to Atlantic City. First you have to decide which presentations or workshops to "play." Some are so popular you can't even get a seat, while others are pitifully neglected. Some will be money-sinks and others will pay off beyond your investment, but attend at least one a year, and use the experience to advance a project you have neglected. Learning alone is slow and lonely.*

So consider attending. *Consider* it. Chances are you will come away with something to enrich your work, and at the very least you'll get a free tote bag.

25
Maintaining Magic

"You do not have to write a whole novel today. You only have to write on the novel today."
—Julia Cameron

Author Iain S. Baird maintained discipline when writing his memoir by reviewing what others had said on the subject of perseverance:

"The process begins by actually sitting down," said Sinclair Lewis. Once you sit down you need to stay in the chair for several hours a day. Ernest Hemingway suggested, "Wearing down seven number two pencils is a good day's work." I simply hung a sign over my desk stating, "Butt in Chair" and tried to get it there on a regular basis.

Five years after receiving a Master of Fine Arts, only about 50 percent of those graduates are still writing. At 10 years, only 10 percent are. How do you maintain the magic? How do you continue to write without any assurance of publication? Without financial remuneration?

Incubation of your writing takes tenacity, an unpredictable amount of time, fierce protection, instinct, and motivation. Giving birth to anything takes a mighty will and a mighty heart. Writers understand this and respect the process wherever it manifests.

"Let's hope we're not going to have another incident like the one with Harry," my husband says cautiously when I tell him three birds have constructed nests within several feet of the house. A baby robin, devoid of feathers, Harry was the lone survivor of a cat's attack on his parents' nest in the purple clematis vine three years ago.

"It won't be like Harry," I say, hoping this is true. There is a timid cardinal in the yellow rosebush that over-climbs the porch; a thrush has made her nursery under the eaves; and a robin has parked her brood on the trellis in the backyard. Each nest contains three eggs, and I have become a bit overinvested in each family. I repeatedly check for a perky tail and a beady eye among the petals to make sure each mother is on the job.

How do you continue to protect your work in a meaningful way when it feels like a lot of sitting? How do you thwart discouragement and intruders? Fend off boredom so your work will flourish, mature, and fly?

Navigating in the Dark

After a reading, I once asked Andrew Miller, the author of *Ingenious Pain*, how he sustained himself through a novel-length work. He explained that when you're writing a novel, or a work of any real length, it's like you're a ship crossing the ocean. At some point you will no longer be able to see either shore. You keep on going, believing that the other shore is there and that if you keep heading toward it, you'll eventually arrive. So how do you keep heading toward that shore you can't see? It may be fairly easy in the light of day, but how about in the dark of doubt, the doldrums of the middle distance?

Run to the stop sign. I'm a runner and I hate it. I only run because it is good for me and I feel better afterward, but I have to trick myself after the first mile in order to continue. So I tell myself I only have to run to the lilac bush or the stop sign on the corner or to the traffic light on Church Circle, and somehow I can run the whole 4 miles that way.

As a writer, it's okay to just run to the stop sign. It's okay to spend a day getting a paragraph down, or just editing. It's *not* okay to beat yourself up for not having produced a new chapter this week. It's okay to spend time reading in preparation for writing. Set small goals and chances are you'll set new ones. Just sit down to read and chances are you will edit. Sit down to edit and chances are you will write.

Get out of the house. According to Deepak Chopra, getting outside to appreciate nature is as beneficial as meditating—in fact, it is a form of meditation. It uniquely links us to a feeling of oneness and well-being that brings you back to the page empowered.

Keep your eyes open for some curiosities. For example, in the acknowledgments of E. Annie Proulx's Pulitzer Prize–winning novel *The Shipping News,* she reveals that without the inspiration of Clifford W. Ashley's book *The Ashley Book of Knots,* which she bought at a yard sale for a quarter, *The Shipping News* would have remained just an idea.

Get to know your colleagues. Besides reading for stimulation and entertainment, try reading biographies of other writers. You'll see how they accomplished their goals and that these are people much like you. They, too, had their dry times, their doubts, their lack of funds, and not only will you understand you are in good company but you will also be able to read how each of those challenges was overcome and be able to apply those antidotes to your own work.

Write your own review. Imagine that your book is finished and in the hands of a reviewer. Write the best possible review—the review of your dreams—and be specific. Not words like "wonderful" but words like "spare, evocative language," or "metaphors that make you see with new eyes things that had become lost in familiarity." Write a review that heralds everything you are trying to do and confirms every strength ever demonstrated in your work. Then write *up* to the review. Hold it as your standard, your benchmark—which is why the specifics are important. Let the review remind you metaphor is your forte, or language, or plot.

More of this, please. Wherever you write, keep reminders of your success around you—frame acceptance letters, paychecks, published work, photographs, notes from a stranger who loved your story, illustrations. Keep the energy in your workspace positive no matter how modest. You want to hold the feeling of possibility as you write, not longing, or even hope.

Can't Put It Down

How do you keep your reader turning pages now that you want to keep writing them? Your story is made up of many elements of craft, but we have said that it is *plot* that keeps the story going because *plot* is what happens in a story, nothing more and nothing less. Exquisite writing in which nothing happens is eventually boring. No matter how caught up a reader is in your characterization, your sense of place, the metaphor of your theme, at some point he's going to get edgy if something doesn't happen.

What happens next? That is the question that leads the reader through.

When you feel lost or you can feel yourself sliding out of focus, stop and ask yourself where you are on the level of both the external and internal conflict and make something happen. Ask: what is the next step I need to take to move my story toward that ultimate resolution?

Imagine that your character wants to regain physical custody of her son. That's the external conflict. The internal subtext is that she wants to regain his trust, his respect. She wants to recover her self-esteem, no matter what the outcome of the custody battle. One conflict takes place in the physical world; she is going to court, she's testifying. The other conflict is taking place in the emotional world; she sees her son turn and follow her with remorse in his eyes when he is led away after the hearing.

One technique to use in any story is to make a character want something as simple as a safety pin or a blanket; to get an appointment or even a classmate's attention. The reader will get hooked wanting that for your character as well. Try going for something small, real, and specific and see what happens. Often your wiser writer inside will find the pattern and the metaphor for you and lead you almost effortlessly where you needed to go on the larger level.

Many first novelists and beginning writers resolve their stories too quickly. They get tired and wrap it up or race toward the end. A novel that was poetic, full of compelling and thought-provoking characterization, suddenly becomes plot-thick. Sometimes you discover that you stopped writing your book or story and what you've been writing is the *summary*.

To slow it down and flesh it out, go deeper. Ask yourself: What am I not saying? What risk am I not taking? What is my character not revealing to himself? What vulnerability is he hiding? What secret is being protected? Force your character to strip away the first superficial layer to greater honesty. Candor in writing, just as in conversation, always makes us sit up and take notice.

If you have lost interest in a character—and characters drive plot—it may be that he has become too one dimensional and in so doing has lost credibility with you. If your character has been portrayed as too good, look for his weakness. If he is despicable, look for the one moment he is vulnerable; expose his humanity.

Lisa Shea does a beautiful job of this in her novel *Hula*. The father has come back from war with a significant head injury. He is violent, full of rage, and an alcoholic. He sometimes puts on a gorilla mask and rubber hands in order to lope about the dinner table snatching food off the plates of his wife and young daughters, stuffing it into the mask as if the gorilla is eating it, making a mess, ruining the meal. The narrator hates this scene, tries in vain to cover her supper with her small hands, and we feel her embarrassment, shame, dismay. We have no sympathy for this inexplicable juvenile behavior until the father finally strips off the mask and walks away with tears in his eyes. Those four words—"tears in his eyes"— change everything. Shea has revealed his humanity.

Another way to keep a story moving is to frame the story in a literal trip or journey like *Canterbury Tales*. Put your characters on a plane or train, or in a car. Think in terms of Cormac McCarthy's *The Road* or Jack Kerouac's *On the Road* or the movie *Little Miss Sunshine*. If you have characters going somewhere, action is required as the story goes along, and eventually they will arrive.

A similar technique is to follow the seasons of the year or the hours in a day, a diary or a school year, a decade, the calendar from one full moon to the next, or the years through high school or college. Use time as your frame, your vehicle for movement.

Move your story forward by raising the stakes. For instance, if I write a story about a woman who loses a child in a miscarriage, you will care. But suppose I tell you that she lost the child six months into her pregnancy and that this child was conceived just before her husband, whom she adored, was killed in a car accident. That this child was her only reason to live through her grief. Now suppose I tell you that her husband was his parents' only child and the child she carried would have been the only heir to a fortune— the only one to carry on the family name. That the mother is already 42. Do you see how the stakes get higher? And when they do, the work becomes more compelling.

Suppose I write that a policeman is shot by an armed robber. Now what if I tell you that he was off duty; unarmed? That he wasn't even supposed to be in the bank that day but was doing a favor, making a deposit for an elderly neighbor. That he could have hidden and been safe, but he purposely drew the gunman's fire to save a small child.

Readers are compelled by suffering but always more by a character who sacrifices, who chooses to suffer. Martyrs have founded entire political movements and religions.

What Have You Got to Lose?

To be compelling, a work should center on someone or something in jeopardy. If you are losing interest in your work and feel directionless, address the question of who stands to lose what. Does a couple stand to lose their marriage? Is a temple going to lose its rabbi? Does a town stand to lose its factory? Is a species in jeopardy? Make the risks clear.

Mystery: Readers love unanswered questions, puzzles, allusions to the fact that nothing is quite what it appears to be. Create a mystery; drop a clue. Look at your story and see if there isn't room for surprise, for something that can reveal itself to be something other than it is. The character who appears to be the kindly minister may rekindle your reader's interest and your own if you give him a hidden past.

Kaboom!: (Also known as, "Bring in a man with a gun.") Make something big happen. This is slightly different than plotting your way toward a climax. You have characters, you like them. You like their problems, their conflicts, where they are headed, but things are a little flat; they're not getting there fast enough. Make. Something. Big. Happen. Something unexpected, something huge. Then let each of your characters react in keeping with their personalities and see what happens.

Research: Arthur Golden, who wrote *Memoirs of a Geisha*, spent years living in Japan, conducting interviews and reading. He explains that writers are drawn to a subject because it interests them, but as you begin to research your subject, you begin to imagine new aspects of your story and feel your imagination sparked. Sometimes the way to move forward is by doing research.

Encore

Chapter 2 noted that going back to your beginning was a good way to find inspiration for your story's end, but it is also a way to keep going when you hit that place a third or halfway through, when your creative engine slips into idle. Go back to the beginning of your book with a paper and pencil and start jotting down the elements you've put in: the woman who was digging in her garden on the first page, the dog down the street that everyone feared, the misdelivered mail left on the counter. Maybe it is a theme you have placed in the text but not developed: a character who was into astrology, someone who was learning sign language.

After you have your list of elements, both tangible things and themes, see if you can put one or more back into the story. Let it come back on stage midway through and see what happens. Not only does the reader like recurrence, just the way we like to hear the melody line of a symphony again and again, often you find you have unwittingly stumbled on a new path to where you were going.

The person learning sign language, a momentary scene you thought had served its purpose, now picks it up again at a place in your book or story where it takes on new significance. Now the reader is beginning to see this character is emotionally mute, or unable to express what needs expressing in other ways in his life. You have the vision again, new directions.

The blueprint for where to go is usually already in the work.

We have had three different outcomes from the bird dramas. Three plump baby robins are crowding the nest on the trellis in the backyard. Mother and father are on a full-time flight schedule keeping them fed. The hatchlings are just beginning to grow feathers on their round little heads, but the fine downy stuff wafts in the breeze, making them resemble little bald men with bad comb-overs.

Under the eaves, a mother still waits. The thrush continues to sit on the nest to protect her project, three new and vulnerable eggs. Inside each, a tiny life struggles to form. When I walk outside and look up at the nest, she stares straight ahead, serious and committed in her effort. Sometimes she turns an eye down at me and I whisper encouragement.

The cardinal mother has lost her battle. Her nest in a bower of buttery yellow roses as big as my hand was torn in half sometime when neither she nor I could protect it. The eggs are gone, not even a broken piece of shell to be found. I don't know which of the cardinals signaling from the nearby holly tree is her. What I do know is that she will build and birth again.

Keep writing. When one project is complete or stalls, start another. Write of jeopardy, suffering, sacrifice, the big event. Make something happen, tell the truth, go on a journey. You are the creator, the parent, the nurturer and protector of your fledgling work. Just sit down. Plan to stay. Just write.

26

Writing Principles for Mind and Heart

"Writing is a hard way to make a living but a good way to make a life."
—Doris Betts

As I walk across the parking lot to my last writing class this semester, my footsteps echo the beat of the mantra in my head: let each student have received what he came for ... but maybe some prayers are on record and don't need repeating.

In reality, however, I fear prayer requires exactitude—like you are assembling DNA and there is only a 1 percent difference between fruit fly and human. If you forget that last piece of genetic code—the envisioning of your request, the gratitude, the allowing— a chuckling God's going to demonstrate what it means to get what you asked for. So sometimes as I hit the brick walkway under the tulip poplars I add the caveat, "in service of the highest for all of us," my cosmic insurance policy in case the meeting of someone's needs, including my own, would not have benefited the whole. It seems to work because as we end the semester tonight, as always, I will take away more than I've given.

Writing is a duet of giving and receiving, and the writing spirit is a generous one. Plumbers spend time and energy learning to fix your pipes. You respect their skill and are grateful for their choice of livelihood when your pipes leak. But writers? Writers want to give you something enormous and impractical, something bigger than any page can contain. Given the means, writers want to give something that will amuse, entertain, last forever, *and* fix your pipes. We can't help it. It's our nature.

Entering the room I greet this group with its impressive professional resumés for the last time; a lawyer with wire-rim glasses who has now begun writing a novel, a harried young mother who has now written her first essay about her kids, a World Bank officer who now has a series of stories about his native India.

"Wow," some of them thought at the initial recitation of accomplishments. Cloaked with degrees and professions, the room stirred with expectations and fears. Tonight they understand that there is no good or bad. There is present and there is elsewhere, there is off-the-mark and authentic. There is courage and there is cliché. There is us, only us, and it is time to take our craft into the world and say goodbye.

My students came to learn to write in the midst of their personal dramas: a dying father, a failing marriage, tender widowhood, 20-something angst, overwhelmed motherhood. What I hope they will begin to realize is that the tools of craft with which they leave can be applied to their lives as well.

Begin where you are, I would tell them. Life, like writing, is an act of faith, similar in what it requires to be authentic. Like a story, life is a revelation. Nothing is as it appears, and while you can choose the characters who will inhabit your story, a character who is all good or all bad isn't credible. Therefore, I would tell them, share your affection without judgment.

Know the stakes, then raise them and, occasionally, make something big happen.

When you get lost in the middle, go back to the beginning and look at what you've given yourselves to work with. Life contains conflict that must be resolved ... in our deepest defenses there is longing.

Show more than you tell, but tell the big secrets. Your relationships will be as compelling as they are honest, as moving as you are vulnerable.

Life contains surprise. It is a work in progress. Revise.

Don't worry about whether the choices you are making are good or bad; be concerned only that they are honest.

Love with abandon, and may the stories you write be shared. May each one be sacred and necessary, an expression of grace, a source of great joy.

Not all of them have figured this out yet, but I hope they do. At the moment they are sad that class is over, anxious that they'll lose momentum, that their stories won't get written, or they'll get written but not read, or read but not published.

I can only tell them what I believe. That we are interesting to each other: not so much what we think, but what we wonder, how we feel, and we should share this.

As the poet Rumi wrote:

From the moment I heard my first story
I started looking for you.

Write for that person, the one looking for you, I suggest. Make a little space and time, celebrate every effort. Trust yourself and trust the process, I remind them as we say goodbye.

You don't have to know where you are going in order to begin.

Appendix A

Suggested Reading List

Bickman, Jack. *The 38 Most Common Fiction Writing Mistakes*. Cincinnati: Writer's Digest Books, 1992.

Cameron, Julia. *The Artist's Way*. New York: Jeremy P. Tarcher/ Putnam, 1992.

Franklin, Jon. *Writing for Story*. New York: Plume/Penguin Group, 1986.

Goldberg, Natalie. *Old Friend from Far Away*. New York: Free Press, 2007.

Klauser, Henriette Anne. *Writing on Both Sides of the Brain*. San Francisco: Harper, 1987.

Lukeman, Noah. *The Plot Thickens*. New York: St. Martin's/ Griffin, 2002.

Moore, Dinty. *The Truth of the Matter*. New York: Pearson Longman, 2007.

Rico, Gabriel Lusser. *Writing the Natural Way*. Los Angeles: J. P. Tarcher, Inc. 1983.

Roorbach, Bill. *Writing Life Stories*. Cincinnati: Story Press/ F & W Publishing, 1998.

Stegner, Wallace. *On Teaching and Writing Fiction*. New York: Penguin, 2002.

Thomas, Abigail. *Thinking About Memoir.* New York: AARP Sterling, 2008.

Wood, Monica. *The Pocket Muse: Endless Inspiration*. Cincinnati: Writer's Digest Books, 2006.

Appendix B

Permissions

index

C

I

J

K

S

T

U

V

W–X–Y–Z